AF540503

Extension and Management in Watershed Development

Authors

Dr. Purushottam is presently a Senior Scientist at IIPR, Kanpur. Doing his M.Sc. from AAI-DU Allahabad and Ph.D. from IARI, New Delhi, he worked with Dr. B.P. Sinha in ICAR-AP Cess funded project for two years. He was selected for ARS-1995 and joined as Scientist (Agril. Ext.) in 1998 at VPKAS, Almora where he worked under NATP project on Watershed Development and TAR (IVLP). He specialized himself in Training and Development (Dip. T & D) in 2006 from ISTD, New Delhi. He has to his credit over 30 publications. Also, he is handling a DBT and NABARD projects as Principal Investigator.

Dr. Baldeo Singh is presently Joint Director (Extension) at IARI, New Delhi. Earlier, he has worked as Lecturer at CSA University; Scientist and Senior. Scientist at ICAR Institute; Head (KVK) of IARI; Principal Scientist, Professor & Head (Agril. Ext.), at IARI since 1970. He has 38 years of professional experience in research, teaching, training, extension and management. He has to his credit over 250 research publications. He has compiled/edited/authored 15 books. Also, he has organized 27 advanced training courses.

Extension and Management in Watershed Development

Purushottam
Baldeo Singh

CONCEPT PUBLISHING COMPANY PVT. LTD.
NEW DELHI-110059

ISBN-13-978-81-8069-685-5

First Published 2010

Published and Printed by

Concept Publishing Company Pvt. Ltd.
Regd. Office :
A/15-16, Commercial Block, Mohan Garden
New Delhi-110059 (India)
Phones : 25351460, 25351794, *Fax* : 091-11-25357109
Email : publishing@conceptpub.com.
Website: www.conceptpub.com

Editorial Office :
H-13, Bali Nagar, New Delhi-110 015, India.

Cataloging in Publication Data--*Courtesy:* D.K. Agencies (P) Ltd. <docinfo@dkagencies.com>

Purushottam.
Extension and management in watershed development / Purushottam, Baldeo Singh.
p. cm.
Originally presented as the first author's thesis (Ph. D.)--Indian Agricultural Research Institute.
Includes bibliographical references (p.).
Includes index.
ISBN 13: 9788180696855

1. Watershed management--India--Rajasthan. 2. Agricultural extension work--India-Rajasthan. 3. Rural development personnel--India--Rajasthan. I. Singh, Baldeo, 1948-, joint author. II. Title.

DDC 333.911609544 22

भारतीय कृषि अनुसंधान संस्थान, नई दिल्ली-110012
INDIAN AGRICULTURAL RESEARCH INSTITUTE
NEW DELHI-110012 (INDIA)

भाकृ अनुप
ICAR

डॉ० एस० ए० पाटिल
निदेशक
Dr. S. A. Patil
Director

Phones : (Off) 25733367, 25843375
(Res.) 25733973, 25846774
Fax. : +91-11-2584 6420
E-mail : director@iati.res.in

Foreword

Rainfed agriculture is complex, diverse, underinvested, risky, vulnerable and distress prone. Any of the programme for the development of rainfed will be worth in the country as about 60 per cent of net-sown area is rainfed that support 40 per cent of population. About 87 per cent area of pulses and minor millets, 77 per cent oil seeds, 66 per cent cotton and cereals are rain dependent, 100 per cent of forest and grazing lands, 80 per cent of apples, mangoes and temperate fruits are unirrigated and 66 per cent livestock is supported by rainfed agro-ecologies. Due to the climatic changes, frequency of extreme weather events like droughts has increased during the past 15 years.

The country gets about 4,000 billion cubic metres of water from the sky out of which only about one-fourth of this is actually usable, as the rest runs off into the sea. Over the last century or so, India's population has quadrupled. The average availability of usable water has correspondingly decreased from about 6,000 cubic metres per capita per day to 1,500 to 1,800 metres per capita per day. The ever increasing groundwater depletion is a major threat to people. Studies have revealed that there is a decrease of 1 ft. to 4 ft. annually in the ground water level. We have to realize the importance of conserving water and take it as our own responsibility to rectify the situation.

Watershed management is the best option for integrated management of resources to alleviate poverty and hunger.

A close look at the watershed programme initiated more than four decades ago in India reveals that the approach has evolved over time from compartmental to integrated and holistic approach for managing the natural resources. The issues of enhancing productivity, sustainability, gender mainstreaming, capacity building, and equity concerns have become important. Common guidelines for convergence, coordination and harmonization of watershed development projects are needed.

I am happy to learn that one of the Research Scholars from, Agricultural Extension Division of Indian Agricultural Research Institute, New Delhi has published his Ph.D. work titled "Extension and Management in Watershed Development" in the form of a book from Concept Publishing Company Pvt. Ltd., New Delhi. The publication is a probe of implementation process of watershed projects from top to bottom. The authors deserve appreciation for their sincere and dedicated efforts in bringing out this valuable publication. I hope the book will be very useful for those associated with research and extension on watershed development projects, specially Government agencies and Non Government Organizations; who have adopted watershed approach for sustainable development of land and water resources in the country.

S.A. Patil
Director
IARI, New Delhi

Preface

The thrust of Indian Agriculture in the post-Green Revolution period is on enhancement of agricultural productivity through sustainable practices. The government has been giving high priority to holistic and sustainable development of rainfed areas based on the watershed approach. To achieve this end Government of India adopted varying guidelines, approaches, objectives as well as financial allocations to undertake watershed development activities in the country. The term watershed has been referred as the highest topographic point from where rainwater gets diverted or divided. It is an area from which all water drains to a common point, making it an interesting unit for managing water and soil resources to enhance agricultural production. The broad objective of watershed approach was the promotion of the overall economic development and improvement of the socio-economic conditions of the resource poor sections of people inhabiting the watershed areas.

A "Common Approach for Watershed Development" was jointly formulated and adopted by the Ministry of Agriculture and the Ministry of Rural Development, Government of India incorporating the strength of their earlier first generation-based watershed programmes. These guidelines have been developed for implementing the National Watershed Development Project for Rainfed Areas (NWDPRA) programme of the Ministry of Agriculture. The restructured NWDPRA provided for decentralization of procedures, flexibility in choice of technology and provisions for active involvement of the watershed community in planning, execution and evaluation of the programme so that the programme becomes sustainable. The NWDPRA was launched in 1990-91 in 25 States and two Union Territories and continues to be implemented during IX Plan. During the IX Plan it was proposed to treat an area of 2.25 million hectares at an estimated cost of Rs. 1030.00 crore.

The critical examination of progress reports of the NWDPRA showed that the project could not deliver the goods as was planned and expected. This study is a probe into the implementation process being followed in government system. It provides the perception of farmers, project personnel, and scientists in selected aspects of watershed development. The study also pinpoints the factors behind the success of Non Government Organization (NGO) in watershed programme.

The study was carried out with sample of size of 190 respondents selected from Central, State, district, watershed, village and NGO level. The respondents were planner, policy makers, scientists, project personnel, contact farmers (*Mitra Kisan*), beneficiaries, non beneficiaries and NGO personnel. At the field level one watershed project 'Bara Padampura' located 35 km from Jaipur in Rajasthan was critically studied. The methods used in the study were structured schedule, case studies, direct observations and content analysis.

The findings of the study had finally pointed to the functioning of *Mitra Kisan*, level of awareness of the watershed programmes among farmers, organizational issues at implementing agency and at the field level, personal policies of project staff, status of trainings at grassroot level, level of people's participation, perception of scientists to the project and reason for the success and failure of NGO in watershed projects. It also gives valuable information on watershed projects in the introductory and review part of the book.

The publication will be helpful to provide insights to the personnel, who are involved in watershed development in the country under various schemes of public and private sectors. It will serve as guidelines to the students and researcher in watershed development.

We gratefully acknowledge the contribution of Dr. Akshayaber Singh, Professor, Water Technology Centre, IARI, New Delhi. We are ever so grateful for the inspiration and encouragement given by the great visionary Dr. Y.P. Singh, Professor and Head; Dr. B.P. Sinha, Head; and Dr. R.P. Singh, Principal Scientist at Agricultural Extension Division, IARI, New Delhi. We record our appreciation to Dr. R. N. Prasad, former ADG (agro-forestry), ICAR and Dr. R.P. Singh, Principal Scientist, Directorate of Maize Research, IARI, New Delhi for their necessary guidance.

The assistance extended by Mr. Sharad Joshi and his team from CE COE DECON a NGO in Chaksu near Jaipur is also acknowledged.

Purushottam
Baldeo Singh

Contents

List of Tables

List of Figures

1 Introduction

India is one of the world's richest country in terms of its water resources. According to the *Worth of Nation*, a publication brought out for Members of Parliament, the average annual precipitation of India is the highest in the world except Latin America. Out of total effective annual precipitation of 350 million hectare metres (mhm.) of water, around 160 are today being lost to the sea as river flows, of the balance 190, about 20 get stored in reservoirs, around 125 as soil moisture and about 45 as ground water (*Vohra, 1995*).

The major problem with our water resource is rainfall that comes pouring down in four months resulting in an extremely uneven availability of water over time and space with floods and droughts occurrence. Development of societies clearly indicates that water had always been a fundamental building factor for the growth of a healthy economy.

The societies that did not have adequate water or could not manage the available water on a substantial basis slowly lost their edge and comparative advantage and faced a gradual decline in course of time. Acquisition and control of water resources has driven communities to migrate since pre-historical times. A U.N. Conference in Beijing warned that we are silently but surely heading towards "water shock" which will dwarf any oil, crisis we have known. Water is indeed as precious as oil, it is mined like any other natural resource (*Times of India*, 1 April, 1996).

Anybody who can solve the problems of water will

be worthy of two Nobel prizes, one for peace and another for science — *Kennedy*.

Changing scenario of environment degradation emphasizes on account of the intensive pressure on its natural resources more than half of the land area in India has become degraded in one form or the other. About 533 million tonnes (16.4 tonnes/ha) of soil is eroded annually of which 29 per cent soil is deposited on surface reservoirs, resulting in the loss of 1-2 per cent of their storage capacity (*Narayan and Prasad, 1989*). Exploitation of natural resources leading to environmental degradation is frequently a result of poverty and lack of agricultural intensification *(Anderson, 1994)*.

The practices of water impounding and using the same for human, crop and livestock production are gradually vanishing. Mixed farming system makes the best use of ecological inputs and can insure against aberrant climate in rainfall area *(Jha, S.K. et al., 1993)*.

In British India water management was essentially a local matter and was in the hands of the community. This changed with the advent of the "modernity". Control over water resources passed from the hands of the community into those of the States. While ownership of natural resources was claimed by the State, management passed into the hands of engineers and bureaucrats. The induction of western engineering ushered in the era of large dams and there was a concomitant decline of traditional forms of small scale, local community managed systems of water harvesting and management. The new projects became symbols of development and came to be regarded as "the temples of modern India" *(in Nehru's famous phrase)*.

Watershed management is an approach for integrated development of any area. The basic consideration in this approach is related to land and water resource management. The production activity though appear secondary but in a real terms the emphasis is on appropriate land use(s) based on the potentiality of land and liking of the farmers. This concept had been very well defined by *(Wetzel, 1957)* at the time when watershed management activities were launched in India. According to him the activities under this programme "embrace all of the land and water areas which contribute run-off to a common point".

The aim of watershed management is to make the area self-sufficient with regard to basic needs such as food, fuel and fodder improvement over the piece meal approach of the past. It is a coordinated multi-disciplinary approach to planning and implementing within the framework of the natural unit of watershed aimed at stabilizing the agro-environmental resource conditions both on and off farm under which farmers operate.

As it is said that second green revolution is possible only through rainfed area that is practiced in India in 100 million hectares and about 67 per cent of total cultivated area. The current approach and strategy for rainfed farming are based on the concept of conservation of rainwater for holistic and integrated development of potential watersheds and promotion through farming systems approach, management of common property resources and augmenting family income and nutrition levels through household production systems.

In India several programmes (Table 1.1) on soil and water conservation were launched and huge money used in the past. On the basis of accumulated experiences the National Watershed Development Project for Rainfed Area (NWDPRA) was started during Seventh Five Year Plan in 99 selected watersheds of the country. This programme was re-structured and lauded in all States during 1990-91 in the light of the experiences gained and lessons learnt. In Eighth Five Year Plan (1992-97) document, the Planning Commission while discussing watershed management made a comment: "In view of the limited success; these programmes should be evaluated for cost effectiveness and replicability ".

> We in the Planning Commission and others concerned have grown more experienced and more

> expert in planning, but the real question is not planning but implementing the plans— I fear we are not quite so expert at implementation as at planning— *Jawahar Lal Nehru.*

There have been doubt whether the watershed or the village should be the unit of planning, but in either case the idea of coordination plan covering all land to command

Table 1.1 : Soil Conservation Programme and their Expenditure

Period	*Highlights*	*Exp. in million*
I Plan (1951-56)	Chain of Soil Conservation, research and demonstration and training centres were established. Ground work for Undertaking soil and water conservation development programmes in the States was laid and works initiated.	16.0
II Plan (1956-61)	All India Soil Survey and Land Use Organisation was established. Model bill on Soil Conservation was circulated to formulate suitable legislation. Emphasis was on Soil Conservation of agriculture land.	233.6
III Plan (1961-66)	Soil Conservation in river valley project was started. Survey of wastelands and ravine lands was initiated.	768.3
Annual Plan (1966-69)	Continued with the programme of III plan.	867.8
IV Plan (1969-74)	The concept of integrated approach and programme planning on the basis of micro and macro watershed was advocated for Soil and Water Conservation. Hydrological gazing stations were established in river valley projects.	1628.9
V plan (1974-79)	Watershed management approach for Soil Conservation received wider attention. Pilot projects on control of shifting cultivation were initiated. State Land Use Board in the States and Union Territories were formed.	2447.0
VI Plan (1980-85)	A National Policy was adopted to use watershed as a unit of land and water resources development and conservation. National Land Use Resource Conservation and Development Commission and National Land Use Board were established.	5482.3
VII Plan (1986-88)	Watershed management was implemented as thrust area. Control of shifting cultivation continued.	5267.0

Source : Khosho and Tejwani, 1993.

watershed acceptance. Integrated watershed development is still an infant and largely at experimental stage. The reporting mechanism is so poor that it is difficult to say with confidence as to how a particular activity has been achieved under each programme *(Vaidyanathan, 1991)*.

Extensive observation shows that whenever these programmes are undertaken by government agencies, the multi-disciplinary aspect of the activities is the first casualty. Unfortunately even single practice or earthwork activities are implemented and often managed by personnel, who are invariably untrained and unoriented and, therefore, uncommitted *(Tejwani, 1992)*.

At research level too, the scenario is not free from confusion. Singh, A. (1991) based on an appraisal survey through interaction with concerned scientists and experts reported on perception at different levels as :

- Watershed Management is no field, it is world's management,
- Develop model for run-off, soil loss and peak estimation,
- Develop procedure for evaluation of development programmes,
- Work out per cent run-off expected in different regions,
- Review the work on watershed management of different regions, and
- Work on small watershed.

These views on one hand reflect confusion and on the other hand identify the areas of gap where "procedures and planning tools" have to be developed. Watershed management is an approach but it has been confused so much. Its adoption in India had been an objective, with the result still we are in the process of trial and error for evolving appropriate procedure for its implementation. Different programmes under this head of activity throughout the country are being implemented on massive scale but the overall scenario is rather in a highly confused state. Sectarian approach and lack of people's participation are the major problems *(Vaidyanathan, 1991)*.

From extension approach point of view, the statement "so far we have followed the highly industrialized countries model for agricultural research strategy. In these countries it is hardly 2-10 per cent population engaged in farming, whereas in India 76 per cent population is dependent on agriculture and in foreseeable future, there is no hope of altering this situation " *(Kanwar, 1991)*. It is quite logical to think that however under such a scenario the technology or the extension approach developed will be applicable in our rural set-up.

The pilot survey conducted for present study in a rainfed urban influenced village of Aravallies hills with 30 farmers reveals (Table 1.2) that majority of farmers were practicing mixed farming in which agriculture with animal husbandry was the most common. People had some common problem like grazing inside agriculture field, lack of land consolidation and irrigation problem etc., but majority (36 %) had said they had no problem for agriculture it may be because of their lack of interest to agriculture. As a potential need they demanded for livestock as major and with agriculture as minor occupation. The majority of farmers were inclined to participate in development programme but they were not clear in their mind how to participate.

Interpretation shows that to ensure participation of people there is a need of specific approach that can fulfil the demand of most of the village people.

Implementation is basically an administrative task needed to put strategy into practice. It also depends on organizational structure and relationship between strategy and structure. Implementation puts decision into action; it uses the commitment and motivation of those who participated in the decision making process. Successful implementation requires the proper use of resources and good management skills. It

Table 1.2 : Farming System and Land Use Activity Scenario in a Rainfed Village

N=30

Sl. No.	*Particulars*	*Percentage*
1.	**Prevailing Farming System/Occupation**	
	Agriculture + animal husbandry	54
	Agriculture	05
	Animal husbandry	14
	Service and business	27
2.	**Major common problem of farmers**	
	Grazing in agriculture field	27
	No consolidation of land	18
	Irrigation	18
	Water logging	05
	Requirement of loans	09
	Nothing	36
3.	**Potentĭal Need**	
	Livestock	31.5
	Agriculture	18
	Agriculture + Animal husbandry	18
	Service and job	09
	Nothing	27
4.	**Participation**	
	Ready for participation in development programme	72

is often used to refer only to the final stage of putting a system into productive operation. It includes pre-installation and post-installation factors.

> I believe all policy statement are paper work. I can write a beautiful policy in one hour, but who is going to adopt that. How are you going to implement it. I believe, in our country, we should think more in the implementation of policies than so much just writing new and new policy papers. You can go on writing, it is good thing to have some guidelines — *M.S. Swaminathan, 1998.*

The primary responsibility for implementation of watershed development programme is with the State government. The Central government provides coordination, technical guidance, training and research inputs in addition to monitoring the progress of implementation and evaluation of the impact of major programmes. The outcome of watershed management programme much depends how effectively they are planned implemented and involves the local people.

Some watershed projects such as Ralegaon Siddhi in Maharashtra and Sukhomajari in Haryana demonstrated very well for integrated natural resource development. There were several factors behind success of these projects. Individual efforts, dedicated leadership, time and flexibility, participatory mode of action were some important one. Whether the replication of these successful projects is possible? Especially when, handled by top-down bureaucratic system of government? If not then what changes required in making the programme successful? To find out the answer of that, it was decided to collect those issues experienced in implementation of a National Watershed Development Project for Rainfed Areas (NWDPRA). An issue is an "important subject" that people discuss or argue. Extension issues are those issues that had played their role at field level and management issues at agency level. Exploration of such issues will provide guidelines for smooth implementation of watershed projects.

In view of above, it was decided to study with following objectives to reflect extension and management issues in overall implementation of the watershed project :

Objectives

1. To examine goals, programme, structure and functioning of watershed projects.

2. To study organizational, technological and socio-economic issues in implementation of watershed project.
3. To study the perception/experiences of project personnel and farmers on selected aspects of watershed development.
4. To compare the issues and suggest appropriate strategy for implementation of project.

Scope of Present Study

This study is an effort to probe into the implementation process being followed in government system. It provides the perception of farmers, project personnel and scientists in selected aspects of watershed development. The study also pinpoints the factors behind the success of Non Government Organisation. It contains the recommendations affecting implementation of watershed project in review part. The study will be a base for discussion in the field of rural development as well as research. The factor related to extension and management will serve the purpose to build the organization and its functioning. The information made available through this study will add to already available knowledge and understanding of watershed development programme.

Limitation of Present Study

A study of this nature which involved analysis of process from policy to programme as well as to implementation, sets number of limitations for a researcher in a short period time. Inspite of these limitations the researcher is to try to overcome some of these constraints by successfully covering respondents from all levels.

The data collected was based on the expressed opinion of respondents. Therefore, the study may not be free from usual biases involved in social investigation. As the study used the ex-post factor as well as participants techniques all the disadvantages and shortcomings that are associated with the techniques and interactional effect of several factors themselves set a limitation for study. However, efforts were made through appropriate statistical analysis to achieve the set objectives of the study so that the essential process involved in watershed development could be understood effectively.

Organization of Report

The study report is organized in five chapters. Chapter I introduces the problem and sets some objectives, its scope and limitations of the work.

A review of work done in this direction has been presented in few sections under Chapter II and has direct relevance to result and discussion.

The methodology adopted being elaborated in Chapter III, presents brief account of research design using procedure of sampling, technique of research used to collect the facts and required analysis of raw data to draw the conclusion.

The findings and discussion run through Chapter IV that provides details on programme, perception/experiences of farmers, project personnel and scientists. It also consists the cases observed in implementation of project and success points behind Non Government Organization in field of watershed development.

The Chapter V presents the summary and conclusions followed by references and schedule for data collection made in report. Appendix is given at the end of this report.

2 Review of Literature

In this chapter efforts are made to review the studies conducted at national and international level related to topic of research.

- Concept of watershed development
- Implementation
- Watershed project implementation
- People's participation
- Non government organization

Concept of Watershed Development

Watzel (1957) conceptually defined watershed as all of the land and water areas, which contribute run-off to a common point.

Reddy and Rao (1967) defined watershed as the entire land area, which drains into a stream from its mouth. The watershed of a stream has not only area but also depth extending from the top of the ridge to the confining geologic strata beneath.

Tolley and Riggs (1967) defined watershed as a drainage area of river, stream, nallah, tank or lake. The watershed has a clear conceptual identity in hydrology and physical geography and is considered an ideal unit for natural resource planning and management.

Tejwani (1977) defined the term watershed as a "Land Area for which water drains to a given point". "Catchment" and "Drainage Basins" are said to be synonymous with "watershed".

ICRISAT's Scientists (1977) were emphatically clear, since water was the first limiting natural factor for crop production in the semi-arid tracts, improving the management of the water and the soil for increasing crops production becomes the primary aim of the watershed based resource utilization research. In rainfed agriculture, only the rain which falls in a given area was used, thus the watershed or catchment was the natural focus for studies of water management in relation to crop production, resource conservation and utilization.

Chakravarty (1978) recognized that watershed is the natural unit for economic management. He opined that small sized watersheds are easily manageable and all treatments can be completed in few years.

Scientists at ICRISAT (1980) stated that a watershed is enclosed by two ridgelines and has a natural drainage outlet. It may encompass areas of thousands of hectares or ten thousands of hectares. For micro-watershed development area of 20-30 hectares is envisaged and the micro-watershed should be developed completely. If only partial development is possible during the initial stage of the project then the upper reaches should be developed first to present untamed incoming water eroding the developed area. The micro watershed can then be inter-linked with other micro-watersheds to create a project area consuming several hundred hectares and thereby incoming and outgoing water can ultimately be controlled for water harvesting or reservoir projects.

Verma (1980) said watershed management is a comprehensive term meaning the rational utilization of land and water resources of a watershed for optimum, production with minimum hazards to natural resources. It relates to soil conservation, proper land use, protection of land against all forms of deterioration, building and maintaining soil fertility, conserving water for farm use, proper management of local water for flood protection and sediment reduction and increasing productivity from all land uses.

Sharma and *Hooja (1981)* referred to the term watershed to an area which has a ridgeline on three sides and whose surplus run-off is drained from drainage point. Watersheds could be as large as 5,000 to 10,000 hectares or even more. The size of watershed to be chosen for land development depend upon the objective of land development planning.

Despande and Reddy (1991) said watershed is a resource region with water, soil topography and biomass as a resource base with water, soil, topography and biomass as its constituents, but the management practice involves human interaction. Hence, it is quite obvious that each watershed would differ in terms of the type of treatment and the impact parameters across the region though the general principle would be the same.

Manage (1994) is in view that watershed management is a holistic approach which aims at optimizing the use of land, water and vegetation in an area to alleviate drought, moderate floods, prevent soil erosion, improve water availability and increase fuel, fodder and agricultural production on a sustained basis.

Implementation

Implementation is the process through which technological, organizational and financial resources are configured together to provide an efficient operating system. In the context of the system design/development life cycle, implementation is often used to refer only to the final stages of putting a system into productive operation, more especially to installation. It includes both pre-installation and post-installation factors.

Project life cycle is generally divided into three phases :

(i) Formulation or planning or pre-implementation or pre-construction;
(ii) Implementation or construction or execution; and

(iii) Operation.

After project is approved detailed, technical design work is undertaken and the implementation or construction is started thereafter. Implementation planning is a stage between the investment decision and start of implementation. During the construction or implementation an effective monitoring system would help in the corrective action being taken whenever deviation occurs in order to ensure that execution. goes in accordance with the implementation plan. However genuine charges are also made during the course of implementation depending the experiences if required.

A formula for implementation has proposed as (*Anonymous, 1964*) :

$$O_S = L_S \times P_L \times P_O$$

Where :

O_S = Organizational support
L_S = Leadership support
P_L = Linkage to existing processes
P_O = Pay off for investing the time

Speidel (1971) and FAO (1980) the given framework as :

1. Origin of the idea,
2. Project preparation,
3. Pre-implementation : Constitution of local body, motivation, community organization, tailoring to make the system more operational, and
4. Implementation : Planning, monitoring, evaluation, continuing execution.

Livingstone (1979) for an implementation of rural development programme takes into consideration the criteria

…on of beneficiaries, State level coordination, multi-pronged approach. Comprehensive area plan could be quite divisible with separate segments capable of independent implementation.

Mukhopadhya, A.K. (1979) in a case study showed that in practice village autonomy is limited and the relationship between the State Government and Panchayat Raj bodies is one of superior and subordinate.

Kohli, Uddesh (1979) found some major component of an implementation plan are: plan for physical work effort, time plan, input resource plan, equipment and order plan, project organisation, responsibilities and systems, plan for construction, inter-linkage with other project activities and plan for project operation.

Waterman, H. (1980) suggests that successful strategy implementation depends on the intervention of 7-S model that are Structure, Strategy, System, Style, Staff, Skills and Subordinate goals.

Bhatta, B.D. (1982) found factors articulated by case study of implementation of decentralized programme are lack of political commitment, lack of coordination between central ministries and agencies and weak personnel strength at district level. It was recommended to make the programme more effective, power must be given to the line agencies functioning at the field level.

Jayaraman, T.K. (1982) for successful implementation, rural development project needs with regard to the various organizational options at a fairly early stage in a multidisciplinary team. It is also necessary to spell out the various tasks assigned to each member of team and to fill key positions with adequately skilled persons.

Boycle, W.P. (1984) for the analysis of project implementation structure calls for a thorough understanding of the culture and subculture of its organizational components.

Hrebeniak and William (1984) said that institutionalization or incorporation of strategy into a system of values, norms and roles will help shape the employees behaviour making it to reach strategic goals. Strategy must be operationalized or translated into specific policies, procedure and rule that will guide planning and decision making. He described four different approaches to strategy implementation depending on size of the problem and availability of time. These are :

- Evolutionary Intervention
- Managerial Intervention
- Sequential Intervention
- Complex Intervention

Hoare, P.W.C. (1984) applied two project implementation strategies. The first worked through a government department and was characterized by strong downward administrative control and few upward communication channels. The second involved : (a) the farmer controls agriculture extension technology, and (b) the formalization of upward communication channels from field to senior management within the government organization.

Honadle, G. (1984) said that three conditions determine the choice of organizational configuration for implementing a rural development project. These are technology to be employed, the ideas and strategies currently in vogue in the donor organization and the political dynamics and capabilities within various segments of the recipient country.

Ramreddy G. and *Hargopal G. (1985)* in a study finds that crucial role is played by the bureaucracy in implementing anti-poverty programmes and the importance of the middleman in project implementation was recognized.

Richter, L. (1985) opined that successful projects require a strong evaluation component and full government commitment. The establishment of an effective mechanism for coordination, careful selection of area, carrying out detailed fact finding surveys affects the implementation.

Morris and *Hough (1987)* said that project are no more concerned only with commercial, technical, organizational and financial aspects but they need to attend the broader social, community, political, environmental, scarce natural resource usage and other aspects affecting and affected by them.

Gow, D.D. and *Mores, E.R. (1988*) proved that project design and implementation are more Art than Science as they do believe in human progress.

Koons, A. S. (1988) observed the causes and solution during project implementation shows that there were different groups of farmers requiring different approaches for communication. In particular, women and men did not benefit equally because of women's relatively low social status, different agricultural roles and activities and gender strategies and perception which project planners did not recognize and for which they did not compensate.

Swannson, E.W. (1988) said that implementation is best thought of as a bridge between design and utilization and that it must be understood in the context of the development process as a whole, over the full life course of the system.

Osterman, D. et al. (1989) puts three objectives for attaining the plan goal are problem awareness, providing awareness of solutions and implementing solutions.

Jasset, E. M. (1990) found the project lacks overall management and coordination and appears to give little consideration to targeting a particular group, despite its initial objective. However the most important question is whether self-help groups (SHG) have been formed as a result of community initiative or they are the consequences of externally assistance. The study concludes that the latter is probably true.

J. Akong and *O. Chitere (1991)* said Participatory Action Research (PAR) is a concept which recognizes the need of continuous research for project implementation and the direct role of the social sciences in the implementation process. PAR involves the practical application of a participant's method of data collection, aimed at introducing positive changes in the community being researched. It is not, therefore, an end in itself but a means through which a change agency and the community can be brought to better mutual understanding for rapid development.

Naidu, V.J. (1992) told that the type of participation, which involves people in formulation, implementation and management of projects and programme have not been practiced in India and such involvement of people calls for a system of planning from the grassroot with a large degree of decentralization.

Oermann, C. (1994) opined two concepts as planning by objectives can be compared with action research. As "Planning by Objectives" (ZOPP) is described as a system of planning a development project where all those concerned with its future implementation create a workshop to discuss core problems and their major causes and to set the target objectives for the project. Whereas "Action Research" is a method of promoting social participation through frequent meetings of development workers with those affected during the course of the project implementation to identify and deal with problems as they arise and maintain long term local interest in the project's progress.

Singh, Y.P. (1995) is of the view that if one wants to study the implementation at village then he should try to know, at the beginning who goes first to village to whom he contacted, and what he discussed.

Morris, Debbie (1996) found out possible factors and barriers considered in designing the implementation strategy.

1. Keep it simple, user friendly and flexible,
2. Come for a top down organizational commitment from more than a single sponsor,
3. Provide choices about whether, when and how to implement especially rewards and recognition, and
4. Create high involvement.

Watershed Project Implementation

Appropriate organizational structure holds the key to successful planning and implementation of multi-sectorial watershed development programme. Planning and implementation accomplished by a multi-disciplinary watershed development team. For each micro-watershed in consultation with the farmers, trained in each village and also the general body of the beneficiaries will be a supervisory committee headed by the Block Pramukh with Pradhans of participating village members and BDO respectively as vice-chairman, conveyor of this committee. *(Hanumanta Rao Guidelines, 1995)*

Krishnamachari, V. T. (1960) said maintenance of bunds should be undertaken in each village. There should be laws defining the responsibility of beneficiaries for constructing and maintaining bunds on their holding and for meeting the proportionate cost of common works.

Contrears, A. (1976) A project is "any activity to which resources are dedicated for the purpose of obtaining benefits" or "a particular method adopted for achieving a specific purpose". It refers to a particular use of resources that is to be evaluated. A project involves inputs (cost) and outputs (benefits). The project becomes something concrete, which can be identified with specific purposes.

Gregerson (1978) incentives provide a policy tool for overcoming the major constraints. The peasant involvement in reforestation and conservation plans and projects; such constraints include lack of awareness of the benefits of such plans and projects, lack of interest in participating due to limited financial appeal, lack of financial and technical capacity, legal difficulties arising from land use problems, and shortcomings in service and marketing infrastructure.

Gupta (1980) in the sequence of watershed development planning opined that one should spend one year on planning, two years in execution and two years on maintenance. After five years the area should be returned to the villagers.

Jaiswal, N.K. (1982) observation of a micro-irrigation project shows that though the project has positive impact but the implementation plan not effectively chalked out and due care has not been taken with regard to time aspect for completing the supporting activities like field channels and development.

Angeles MS-de-Los (1985) a resource conservation project such as agro-forestry entails the recognition of the inter-relationship between the physical, economic and institutional considerations in project implementation.

Jaiswal et al. (1985) reported that 92 per cent beneficiary farmers were aware of activities like contour bunding and 67 per cent knew about tree plantation while 31 per cent knew about gully plugging. Other activities like sericulture and pasture development were known to 10 and 8 per cent beneficiary farmers respectively.

Sander, S. (1985) how much do we know of the farmers concept and attitudes to soil erosion, what is required to motivate farmers to apply soil conservation practice? And what is needed to make farmers continue with conservation and maintenance works are already installed.

In the proceedings of National Seminar on Soil Conservation and Watershed Management *(1985)* reveal "Although plan is often well integrated, implementation is not, therefore, introduction of project officer or catchment area commissioner after B.B. Vohra model is recommended for field level coordination and integrated work."

Bali (1987) said that soil and water conservation policy initiatives would become a reality only if the present programme oriented planning is replaced by integrated agro-industrial watershed projects breaking the presently non-coordinating programme and departmental agencies and converting them into multidisciplined integrated area projects. Biomass processing pattern should become essential feature to increase rural income, full employment and checking of rural-urban employment.

Reddy and *Walkar (1987)* reported that big farmers had more favourable perception than small farmers towards all the three components of watershed management viz., soil and water conservation, improved dry farming and non-arable land development. The study further revealed that 57 per cent farmers perceived the soil and water conservation practices and non-arable land treatment practices respectively as useful.

Suelzer, R. and *Sharma K. (1987)* the crucial point in a watershed programme was to create an atmosphere during village workshop in which assessment of problems and opportunities was to become more important than the development programme. The whole process concentrated on the micro-perspective, the detailed approach was how to ascertain a dialectical interaction of the villagers with external "change agents" assessing which of these in with their own situation and their objectivity and perception.

Singh, Katar (1988) in managing dry land watershed programme some weaknesses are identified as lack of appropriate mechanism for enlisting people's participation, omission of animal husbandry activities and paucity of studies to determine farm profitability of different technologies.

Rao et al. (1988) revealed that 62 per cent of marginal, 66.6 per cent small, 71.4 per cent medium and 57.2 per cent large farmers had favourable perception of usefulness of watershed technology.

Singh, R. (1994) an analysis of NWDPRA shows that more attention was paid to water conservation work than soil conservation work. The area irrigated by the concerned water is higher than all other improved irrigation resources in the study area.

Siddaramath (1991) a study shows favourable attitude of 55 per cent farmers towards watershed management programme and 5 out of 11 majority (89-100%) of the farmers has adopted practices.

Bagchee, A. and *Bagchee, S. (1992)* states the study concludes that institutional development (locally acceptable arrangements for sharing the costs and benefits of the projects) is important as the physical development (afforestation, construction of bunds etc.) of the watershed, but is generally neglected aspect of watershed development programme of the government.

Judson (1992) and Napier et al. (1994) found that effective implementation of conservation measures is impeded less by physical and biological constraints than by socio-economic and policy factors.

Singh et al. (1992) suggested that in a project where the components are mutually interdependent, it could provide a fragmented approach to project implementation. In Kándi project of Punjab, the calculation of separate economic rate of return for each component reinforced a tendency for line departments to pursue their separate components with little preference to the activities of other departments.

White, T.A. and *Quinn, R. M. (1992)* put forth few points as a lesson drawn from Kandi watershed project as :

- That irrigation need not be strategy point of the project implementation.
- Rehabilitate the ecosystem requires a project based, on much longer time frame.

Sombatpaint, S. et al. (1993) success in soil conservation implementation requires an understanding of the stages of farmer's mind, perception-attitude-acceptance-adoption and whether they are ready for soil conservation practice. Interviewing in some localities in Thailand indicated that the more progressive farmers had better perceptions of the causes and effects of land degradation and how to apply corrective measures. In a less prosperous area with high land degradation potential, only one out 240 farmers admitted that soil erosion was a problem.

Joshi, A.L. (1994) observed that one of the main problem with our past efforts in soil conservation and watershed management was the lack of input from the users or local people. The technology applied did not take into account the people's perception of the problems and their solutions.

He also observed that soil conservation programmes are more likely to be successfully implemented if they are directly linked to economic benefits to local farmers.

Krishnappa and Hedge (1994) a holistic approach to resource conservation observed the following hurdles and drawbacks in implementing the programmes in watershed areas :

1. Imposing physical targets beyond the implementing capacity of the manpower in stipulated time,
2. Inadequate institutional support,
3. Non-involvement of weaker sections,
4. Lack of infrastructure facilities to impart the training,
5. Absence of effective monitoring and concurrent evaluation,
6. Non-involvement of local statutory institutions,
7. Sectarian disparity in financial procedures,
8. Frequent transfers,
9. Posting of non-technical and uninterested staff.

Ram Babu and B.L. Dhayani (1994) observed that planning is based on poor benchmark database, more so, when nodal agency is forest department. Most of the programmes except Operational Research Projects (ORP) bench mark survey were either not carried out or not analyzed from the watershed management perspective due to lack of trained manpower or little understanding of its importance.

They also found coordination between line department was better when development commissioner or district collector works as a nodal agency, weak coordination between line departments results in independent planning for each watershed by respective department.

Narashimhan, B. (1994) in connection with appropriate land use said that the effectiveness of the intervention would depend on the community wisdom and upgradation of the current knowledge and skills. He observed the following parameters of intervention, land use, technology, cost, time frame and returns. The major problem with the modern governmental institutions is the fragmentation of decision making justified by functionalization and expertise building which lead to dominance of sectarian concerns and strategies.

Purohit, S.D. (1994) in a impact study of NWDPRA in two watershed in Ajmer and Banswara shows slight increase in labour utilization on the beneficiary farms. The net income of beneficiary registered an increase of 24 per cent as compared with only 5 per cent for non-beneficiary.

Sanghi (1994) found few constraints in adoption of indigenous soil and water conservation practices such as lack of finance, dispute over demarcation of ownership boundaries, difficulty in organizing group action, lack of availability of stones, short term tenure system, impact of changing scenario in rural areas.

Hazare, Anna (1995) found that government schemes in constructing percolation tanks to ensure groundwater recharge was not successful because of lack of interest and theoretical knowledge of the people.

Anonymous (1995) states that a very small percentage of funds (only about 20 % of the money allotted) reaches to poors. But they are unable to take any action. There is reason for this :

(1) No meaningful concurrent monitoring of the programme based on sound methodology has been evolved.
(2) Lack of will to take punitive action against the corrupt and inefficient officials.

Prasad, Y. Esworpa et al. (1996) recommendation on strategies for diffusion of technologies in a watershed area shows : that recommended technologies should be made available through *Mitra Kisans*, popular dailies, leaflets, journals and other mass media channels like Radio and T.V. and more ideal demonstration plots should be laid in watershed areas.

Upadhyay, A.P. and *S. Intodiya (1995)* in reaction of farmers about watershed development programme on crop production shows that the programme have impact (60.53%) and no impact (39.47%) both. The free inputs (98.55%) supply for the impact building was the main aim than the motivation and technical advice.

People's Participation

People's participation has been emphasized in India since the inception of economic planning. The First Plan viewed people's participation as a principal force behind Indian planning. The Second Plan considered popular participation as an indispensable tool of mobilizing resources and to achieve the targets. The Third Plan advocated that people's participation is essential to galvanize local resources to construct village roads minor irrigation works, water supply and drainage etc. The Fourth Plan talked of "creating a milieu in which the small man who has so far had little opportunity of perceiving and participating is the immense possibilities of growth to organized effort to put in his best to the interest of a higher standard of life for himself." The Fifth Plan considered public participation as an essential requisite for proper implementation of Plan programmes. The Sixth Plan talked of organizing people's power and their fullest participation. The Seventh Plan was equally vehement in emphasizing the role of people's participation in development. *(Naidu, V.J., 1992)*

The goal of development is no longer defined in terms of increments to physical quantities of goods but in terms of development of people. In the context of development planning, participation means involvement of the beneficiaries in decision-making, planning, implementing and evaluation of projects and programme.

Schumacher, E.F. (1973) expresses that development does not start with goods but it starts with people and their education, organization and discipline. An entirely new system of thought is needed, a system based on attention to people and not primarily an attention to goods, for goods will look themselves.

Muthaya and Ranga (1980) reported that positive attitude is necessary for the people to participate in groups activities.

Wandersman (1981) reported a positive relationship between the psychological character of the individual and their participation in community processes.

Santhanam et al. (1982) found that aspects like self-esteem personal efficacy, extraversion, need for achievement, internal conviction to participate in social activities were responsible for ensuring people's participation.

Wyekoff, J.B. (1985) support from ultimate beneficiaries is sufficient condition for successful project implementation. In the Fifth Plan of India it is said "If the people are convinced that the basic objective of the Plan is social justice, they will be interested in programme and will execute with their cooperation. No Plan can ignore the deep-rooted sentiments of our people for greater equity.

Choudhary, Q. A. (1986) said traditional attitudes and illiteracy are handicaps for the rural poor's participation in small-scale water sector projects.

Singh, Katar (1986) man is the cause and consequences of development. The purpose of development is man. It is the creation of conditions both material and spiritual, which enable man, individual and species, to be at his best. There are at least three basic elements, which are considered to constitute the "true" meaning of development of life sustenance, self-respect and freedom.

Rej (1987) in Sub-Saharan Africa, the main elements

identified for participatory conservation programme included the selection of simple but efficient technology which made use of indigenous conservation techniques and were popular among the people and involved them in experimentation.

Zoghby, S.E.L. et al. (1987) Government organization should do in priority for increasing participation at the local level with addressing important need of the community, allow members to express their ideas and discuss their problems, organize meetings and group discussions to educate people and allow whole community to benefit from activities.

Vanden Van (1988) views implementation of decision is much faster with a participatory style.

Anonymous (1991) views the review and interaction corroboration with the conclusion drawn on lacuna and constraints in watershed management programmes are as follows :

1. Lack of understanding of basics,
2. Poor project planning and implementation,
3. Non-availability and miss-utilization of funds,
4. Misinterpretation of working,
5. Lack of coordination and cooperation,
6. Lack of people's participation,
7. Plethora of schemes, and
8. Inadequate monitoring and evaluation.

In 51st annual conference of the Indian Society of Agril. Eco. held in 1991 at Hyderabad in all 40 papers were submitted focusing on economic analysis and functioning of watershed projects *(Singh, R. P., 1991)* brought out following facts after reviewing all the papers :

(i) There is lack of adequate information about the resources and requirement of the people of the watershed area for proper planning of the project.

(ii) People and location are the two most important factors that should be considered while designing the project.

(iii) Improvement in project is possible by considering the needs of the people and major constraints faced by them.

(iv) The sustenance of the flow of benefits as well as impact parameters has a direct function of community participation.

(v) Weakness of the programme includes lack of proper comprehensive plan, lack of coordination among departments, lack of involvement of local people and organisation, lack of motivated staff and flexibility in the use of funds.

(vi) Active people's participation in watershed development depends on expected private benefit and costs of participation, organisation of farmers in small groups, good local leadership, existence and enforcement of rules for fair and equitable benefits from collective action, involvement of non governmental organisation in organising training and motivating the farmers, besides willingness and ability of the government to provide financial and technical support.

Naidu, V.J. (1992) views low level of awareness was due to non-awareness to programme, caste and ethnic differences, bureaucrats tendency to ignore the poors and in promoting participation, appropriate education, communication, persuasion and demonstrations were important factor in promoting involvement.

Joshi, A.L. (1994) participation begins in the initial stages of designing and planning through the implementation, monitoring and evaluation stages and lasts up to the continuous follow up stage of maintenance and benefit sharing among participatory groups.

Decentralization and community forestry have been two major policies of government that support the people's participation in soil conservation programme.

The important factors that contributed in successful people's participation are :

(i) Transparent project programme, budget, plans, implementation procedures, benefit sharing mechanism, and
(ii) Integration of wide variety of soil conservation and watershed management activities institutionalization of the follow-up programme.

Srinivasaramanujan, T.C.A. (1994) states in order to secure maximum participation of the people in carrying programmes or a particular activity, development agency to seek answers the following :

- What do the people think about development?
- What kind of development they want or anticipate?
- What they know about the resources they are endowed with?
- In what way do the people intended to make use of such resources?
- What do the people think that their community can do?
- What do the people expect from development agency?

Singh and Verma (1995) reported for poor performance of vegetative barrier on arable land. The progress was not satisfactory because of :

(a) The soil was badly infested by termites,
(b) Vetiver species provided by the project were not found suitable to the local conditions, and

(c) Least interest shown by farmers in planting and proper care.

On the whole the main emphasis of the project has been noticed on the supply of inputs like HYV seeds, fertilizers and equipments. People's participation in planting trees was limited to the paid employment.

Non Government Organization (NGO)

Government system is efficient in book- keeping, accounting and technology where NGO system is good in inspiring people and human engineering to organise them. They also possess dedication and commitment for social services. The local people have cumulated wisdom, skills and knowledge of the production environment encompassing land, water, vegetation etc. "When all these GO, NGO and watershed community join hands with the object of enabling the local communities to organise themselves and develop self-help culture, the sustainable development takes place." *(Reference in WARSA-6 Regional Review of NWDPRA, p. 48)*

Schnedder et al. (1973) found that organizational climate can have a major influence on motivation, productivity and job satisfaction by creating certain kinds of expectations about what consequence will follow from different action.

Mae Neil (1980) found the education purpose of many voluntary organizations are not always identifiable or even articulated, most organizations have some educational purpose.

Draper (1984) found voluntary organisations do have their own style of functioning, which ensures success of the programmes which even government cannot do. The works of NGOs have always been closely linked to adult education, social work, community development, social action and the training of both by volunteers and professionals.

Brij Bhushan (1994) reported that voluntary work is the

only true measure of the inner strength of a society because it embodies a certain degree of social commitment without which no society can sustain itself.

Dey, B.K. (1994) found that people are better motivated and work with single minded devotion and dedication if they are asked to do what they believe in within the overall framework of organization's holistic belief. These in turn regularize that there is a fusion of mission of the organization, on the one hand and individual on the other hand.

3 Methods and Techniques

This chapter presents a description of the methods and procedure followed in conducting the study consisting of the research design, locale of study and selection of respondents, devices used for collection of data and measures of analysis for the data. Looking into the problem of study the methodology slightly modified with a view to collect the authentic information on the issues covered in the study.

Research & Design

Before deciding the problem on watershed development, a pilot study was conducted which was based on results of pilot survey and thereafter the technical programme was finalized. Since the present study is intended to investigate the issues of extension and management in implementing the watershed projects, the selection of respondents had been done from different categories for facilitating the investigation. The categories of respondents consisted farmers and their representatives, project personnel, scientists, policy makers and NGO personnel. The multi-stage sampling was used for categorization of population under study.

Locale of Study and Selection of Respondents

Review of Information of Project

To review about the project, informations were collected from nodal agency at national level responsible for implementation of project. Relevant guidelines and reports were collected from this source. During these process purposively informal discussions were held about the project from 15 top level planners and senior officials.

Selection of Watershed Project

The Rajasthan State was grouped into 10 agro-climatic zones, 5 circles and 17 divisions to implement the programme. The divisions have further divided into units. Thus, total 80 units and 196 watershed projects were in the State.

Jaipur was one circle headed by joint director, had 4 divisions namely Jaipur, Sikar, Bharatpur and Bikaner. Further, Jaipur division had two units i.e., Jaipur and Alwar. The State level officials had suggested that district Jaipur (Fig. 3.1) is the representative of most of the areas of Rajasthan. The 5 blocks of Jaipur named as Duda, Dausa, Phaggi, Chaksu and Jobner had an average 20.54 per cent of its arable area under assured means of irrigation that is why these blocks comes under the present watershed programme. There were 6 watersheds in Jaipur district. Out of these one watershed project i.e., Bara Padampura located in block Chaksu was selected under study. Bara Padampura (popularly called Padampura) was located at 35 km. from Jaipur on Jaipur-Tonk Road. The watershed was easily approachable from Jaipur and was under the periphery of Durgapura Research Station of Rajasthan Agriculture University. The agencies like Forest Department, DRDA and NGOs were also working in the region. The selected watershed had highest geographical area and watershed was neither ranked at the top nor at the bottom in its overall performance in the State. These were some criteria considered in selection of project at field level.

Selection of Farmers

In the beginning Padampura watershed project consists 26 villages but at the period of study it had 33 villages. The

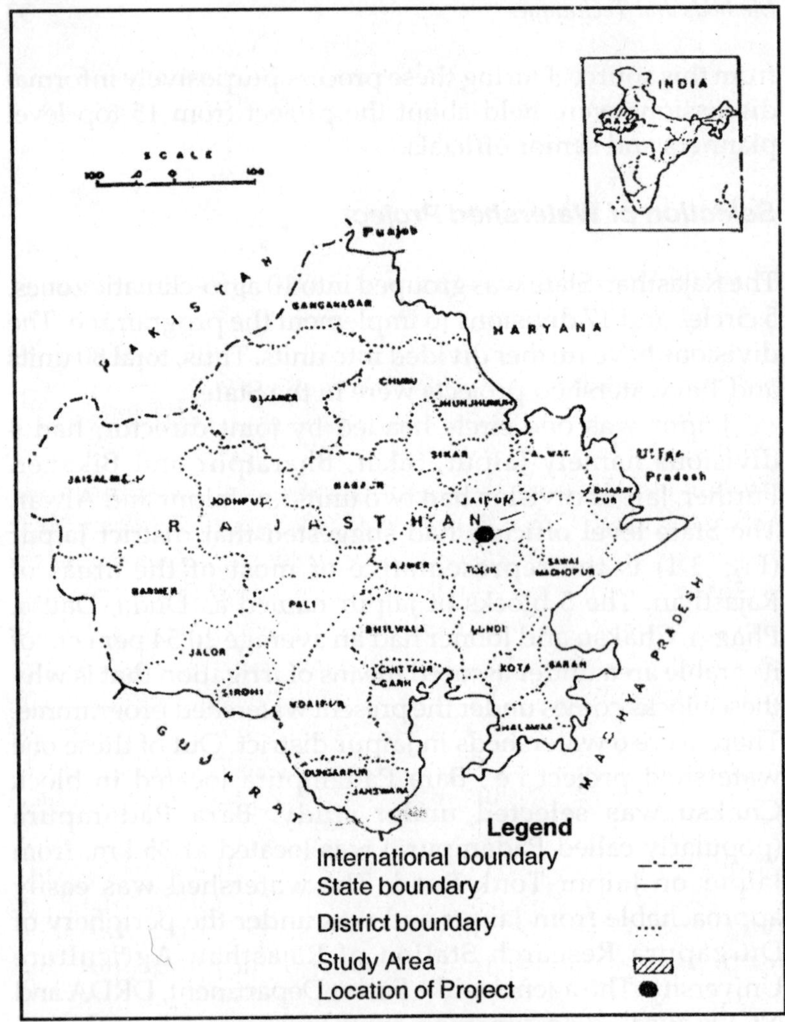

Fig. 3.1 : Study Area of Rajasthan

watershed area was broadly divided into head and tail. The head portion is upper portion (up land) of a drainage line whereas the tail portion is lower. Concentration of activities was in lower portion because of intense soil erosion problem. Based on these facts, the watershed was broadly divided into three micro-watersheds. From each micro-watershed, 2 villages were selected randomly. Thus, from the selected six villages 40 farmers were contacted. The names of persons who had worked under the watershed project were collected from project personnel. One category of contacted farmers (10) were key informants as *mitra kisan* of the project. The next category was those farmers (30) benefited or not benefited from the project activities.

Selection of Project Personnel from State Departments

The State department personnel involved in different positions in the watershed project were selected. One watershed had five permanent employee. In Rajasthan it was reported that satisfactory progress is being made under these projects. With this reason it was decided to study a watershed at field level in Rajasthan taking into account all ten (10) project personnel worked for or working in watershed as a member of multidisciplinary team, or as training personnel associated with project. So,10 personnel who were involved in the watershed project of Jaipur district were selected and interviewed for the purpose. Since the selection of project personnel from one or two watersheds could not serve the purpose, the project personnel of other watersheds were included. The researcher was sent to attend the workshop on watershed management organized by the State department in collaboration with a NGO at Ranchi (Bihar) and made attempt to collect information from a group of 70 project personnel attending the workshop. Thus it was done purposively to have national scenario of the issues under the study. Further the reason behind this was that the proceedings of regional review of NWDPRA showed that Bihar was the State where the project did not make any breakthrough at field level in comparison to Rajasthan.

Selection of Scientists

To know the perception of researchers, data were collected from 45 agriculture scientists/experts who worked in the field of soil and water conservation under different institutions of ICAR and SAUs. These people were not directly involved in project implementation but in development of watershed approach they had played significant role. The idea of contacting of this group was to know the nature of feedback they had received about the project and their opinion/suggestions for the programme. The respondents were purposively contacted at a five-day international conference on soil and water conservation organised at New Delhi.

Selection of Personnel from NGO

It is said that NGO were more successful in watershed projects. To probe this contention it was decided to select a NGO preferably from the same area where implementation procedure was studied at field level. Considering these facts one NGO known as Ce Coe Decon (Agro-action) located in selected watershed periphery which was pioneer in the field of soil and water conservation with good infrastructure and manpower, only ten persons of different categories were identified and chosen for this purpose.

Research Methods and Techniques

To collect the information and probe the objectives under study, a few set methods and techniques were used as :

Sl. No.	*Categories*	*Population*
1.	Planners and top level officials	15
2.	Farmers and their representatives of watershed project	40
3.	Project personnel at State and watershed level	80
4.	Scientists involved in soil and water conservation research	45
5.	NGO personnel to know the reasons for success	10
	Total	190

- Case study method
- Interviews : individual and group

- Participant and non-participant observation
- Cross checking of information
- Content analysis

Case Study Method of Research

Case study method was adopted at watershed level to know the implementation procedures practiced. Case study is "an empirical inquiry that investigates a contemporary phenomena within its real life contest, not clearly evident and in which multiple source of evidence are used *(Yin, 1984)*. In general, the case study method is preferred to other methods when the researcher is interested in answering "Why, How and What" rather than predicting the relations to be found. Here researcher has little control over the factors that affect the phenomenon to be studied. Of the four types of commonly used case study designs, the author chosen the holistic multiple case design. In the present study *case study* was adopted for collection of information from farmers and their representative to know the process of watershed project implementation which was followed and reasons of success behind the Non Government Organization.

Structured Interview Schedule

This is man's oldest and most used device for obtaining information. The structured interview schedule with open-ended questions was used for the purpose. Some informations such as reasons for changes in behaviours, intention and attitude can best be studied with open-end questions *(Kerlinger, 1983)*. Funnel type of questions were also used. Actually this is a set of questions directed towards getting information on a single important topic or a single set of related topics. The funnel starts with a broad question and narrows down progressively to the important specific points. The open-ended questions were prepared for all categories of respondents.

The schedule of data collection was circulated amongst

agriculture scientists and project personnel of Bihar in two separate seminars/workshops organized at New Delhi and Ranchi, respectively. The respondent returned the same after filling in a day or next day. About 90 per cent project personnel of Bihar and 50 per cent agriculture scientists took up the request seriously and rest were indifferent, as they did not return the schedule. The scientists who did not respond, few of them argued that they have no concern to development work and seminar/rest time is not suitable platform for data collection and also researcher can blackmail with the facts to be given in schedule. It was also noted that copying of information was practiced in few project personnel's responses.

Participant and Non–participant Observation

The participants observation method was used for few project personnel associated with selected watershed. Farmers and NGO personnel were interviewed on various aspects. Non-participants observations made at the meeting/training sessions between project staff and farmers, discussion at field visit by project staff, hearing the staff, farmers gossips at leisure time in offices, village grocer's store, tea shops and moving on the way. Similarly, relevant talks and statements of farmers connected with project problem were also overheard in course of stay at village and NGO were recorded.

Content Analysis

The content analysis of following documents was carried out. These sources have concerns to watershed projects under study.

(i) Watershed Areas Rainfed Agriculture System Approach (WARSA) series of NWDPRA. This includes WARSA Guidelines, WARSA regional review report, WARSA plant nursery raising etc.

(ii) Reports of DPAP and DDP programme from Ministry of Rural Areas and Employment, Government of India.
(iii) Hanumanta Rao Guidelines of area development on watershed approach from Wasteland Development Board of Ministry of Rural Areas and Employment, Government of India.
(iv) Annual Reports and reports on low cost indigenous technology of Ministry of Forest and Environment, Ministry of Water Resources and Central Water Commission.
(v) Magazines, Journals, Newspapers cuttings.
(vi) Pocket diary writing.

Cross Checking of Facts

Often situation arose in which facts concerning the same matter collected from diverse sources were of conflicting nature or ran counter to expectations. Therefore, to ascertain the correct situation, cross checking of the facts was resorted to. This technique was frequently used among farmers, *mitra kisan* and project personnel to know the correct implementation procedure followed.

Analysis, Interpretation of Data and Writing the Report

In the analysis of data, at the first stage classification and tabulation methods were used for the purpose. The responses from schedule were taken on master sheets and the content of responses classified in groups with their similarity and dissimilarity. The total number of responses fall in each category were separately noted, thus the frequencies were counted down. The groups having the highest score were given priority putting in top at the time of tabulation. The percentages in relation to total number of respondents were calculated for interpretation of results. The ranking of responses was also done to show the importance of factors.

The information collected as participant observations and non-participant observations were both qualitative and quantitative in nature. The qualitative data were critically analyzed and continuously refined by rewriting in systematic way, so that these could give correct message.

In writing the report, first of all, the sections and chapters to be written were finalized in consultation with the members of research advisory committee. Subsequently, detailed outline was prepared and writing was carried out in proper sequence.

4 Results and Discussions

This chapter presents the results and discussions based on analyzed data. These are presented according to the objectives and described under the following seven major heads :

1. Goals, programme, structure and functioning of watershed project,
2. Awareness of farmers about watershed project and its activities,
3. Organizational, technological and socio-economic issues in implementation of project,
4. Perception/experiences of project personnel on selected aspects of watershed project,
5. Issues of watershed management as perceived by the scientists,
6. Performance of Non Government Organization (NGO) in watershed programme–a case., and
7. Comparison of issues.

1. Goals, Programme, Structure, and Functioning of Watershed Project

Watershed approach has been followed in India since early sixties with basic aim at controlling siltation in reservoirs or mitigating of floods. Subsequently, after announcement of a new 20-point development programme in the year 1982, this approach was adapted as a national strategy for integrated and comprehensive development of rainfed areas. The National Watershed Development Project for Rainfed Areas (NWDPRA) was initiated during Seventh Plan covering 99 districts in 16 States. Its Eighth Plan version was radically different after removing many defects. The programme later on covered twenty-five States and two Union Territories. A total of 2,554 projects covering 4.3 million ha area with Rs. 100 crore expenditure was sanctioned in Eighth Plan. It was assumed that programme would create models of scientific land use through development of integrated farming system on the principle of watershed management in each development block where less than 30 per cent arable area was under assured means of irrigation. In these blocks, a group of villages falling within a selected micro-watershed and land owners of watershed boundary were identified.

Goal of the Watershed Project

The goal of NWDPRA project was to develop the natural resource base, sustain its productivity, and improve the standard of living of millions of poor farmers and landless labours and endeavour for restoration of ecological balance. To achieve this goal, the following objectives were set up :

- Conservation, upgradation and utilization of natural endowments like land, water, plant, animal, and human resources in a harmonious and integrated manner.
- Generation of massive employment.
- Improvement of production environment and restoration of ecological balance.
- Reduction of inequalities between irrigated and rainfed areas.
- Enhancement of cash flow through increased casual employment, marketable surplus of agriculture and dairy produce.

Programme of Watershed Project

A comprehensive project guideline of watershed development programme was developed in consultation with ICAR scientists, expertise available with State departments and NGOs. Valuable items incorporated from the model watershed projects of Sixth Five Year Plan were based on sustainable farming system, integrated watershed management and household production system. The inter-relationship among these components and sub-components would be treated as a unit of development. To ensure proper and integrated development of arable and non-arable land, and drainage lines, conservation and production measures would be used for the project and these would heavily rely on low cost vegetative conservation measures in place of costly engineering structure. *In situ* moisture conservation to green the entire area was major pursuit of the project. Production measures in arable and non-arable lands would include crop development, pasture development, agroforestry, silvipasture, sericulture etc. The measures for drainage line treatment such as networks of ponds, stabilization of nala banks with vegetative barriers were used. To regulate the livestock population and enhance their productivity, livestock population control through castration and health care were also undertaken.

There were 36 physical activities of different nature under the project. For each activity, the total cost was decided in programme guidelines. The average unit cost as a whole in plain area was Rs. 3,500 per hectare including Rs. 500 for management. To qualify for plain area, the watersheds need 75 per cent of its area less than 8 per cent slope. During the entire project period, no individual farming family would get subsidized input for demonstrations and subsidies including dugwells, and implements above Rs. 5,000. In principle the project envisages that there would be some financial contribution for work in private landholding from the beneficiaries, so that they should not perceive the project as government exercise. In this way, broadly, the project cost was divided into eight heads i.e. as survey and field investigation 10 per cent , conservation measures 30 per cent, production measures 30 per cent, training 10 per cent, establishment and management cost 10 per cent, research support 5 per cent, infrastructure cost 2.5 per cent, and reserve fund 2.5 per cent.

The project was financed by Government of India with 75 per cent grant in aid and 25 per cent loan to State Government with internal built-in monitoring and external monitoring and evaluation by professional bodies, the NGOs have also been involved. Informations documented at watershed, block and State levels in registers and were fed into computer. The coordination with National Informatics Centre (NIC) at State and Centre for reporting was developed. Quarterly and annual reports were furnished by watershed development team to State and Central Government. The format for reports was decided.

Organisational Structure of Project

Appropriate organisational structure Fig. 4.1 holds the key to successful planning and implementation of the multi-sectorial watershed development projects. Fig. 4.2 shows that Rainfed Farming Division under Department of Agriculture and Cooperation in Ministry of Agriculture is the central agency responsible for formulation of guidelines, release of funds and monitoring and evaluation of the project. At State level, State nodal agency is responsible for implementation of project. These agencies vary from State to State. In Rajasthan such agency was soil and water conservation department. Other concerned departments help in policy decisions at State level. The Director of soil and water conservation was the implementing head assisted by two additional directors at State level. These additional directors were further assisted by joint directors of the circle. The circle was further divided into divisions and deputy directors were responsible for each division. Thus, 17 divisions were existing

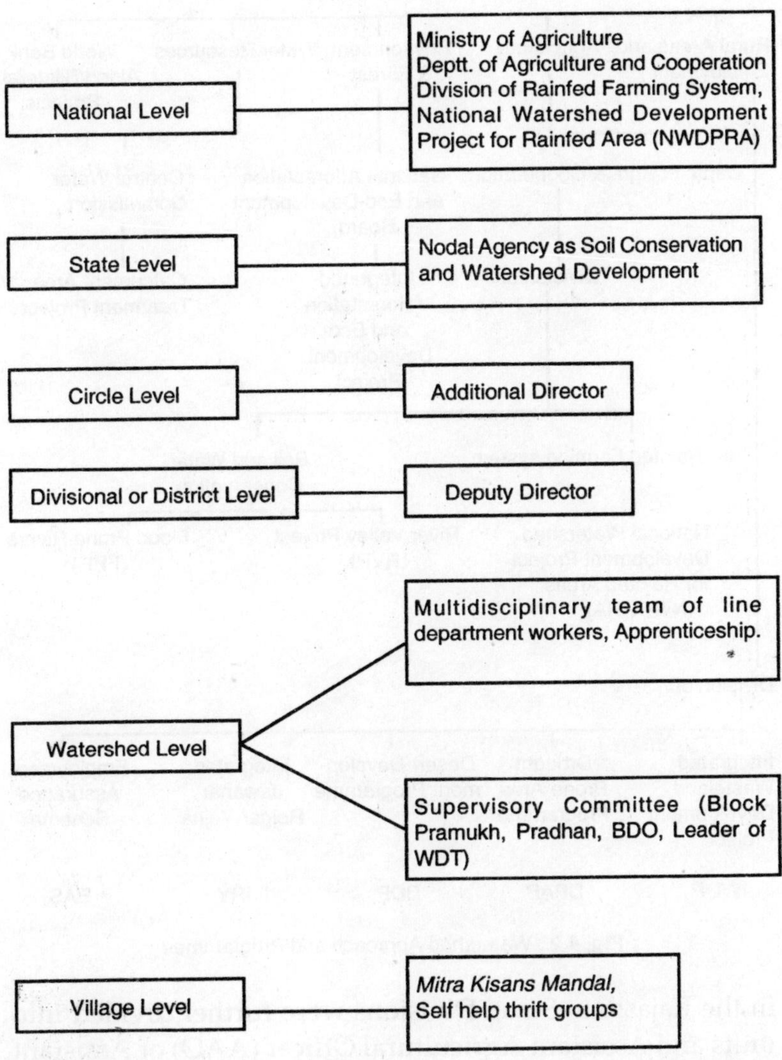

Fig 4.1 : Organisational Chart

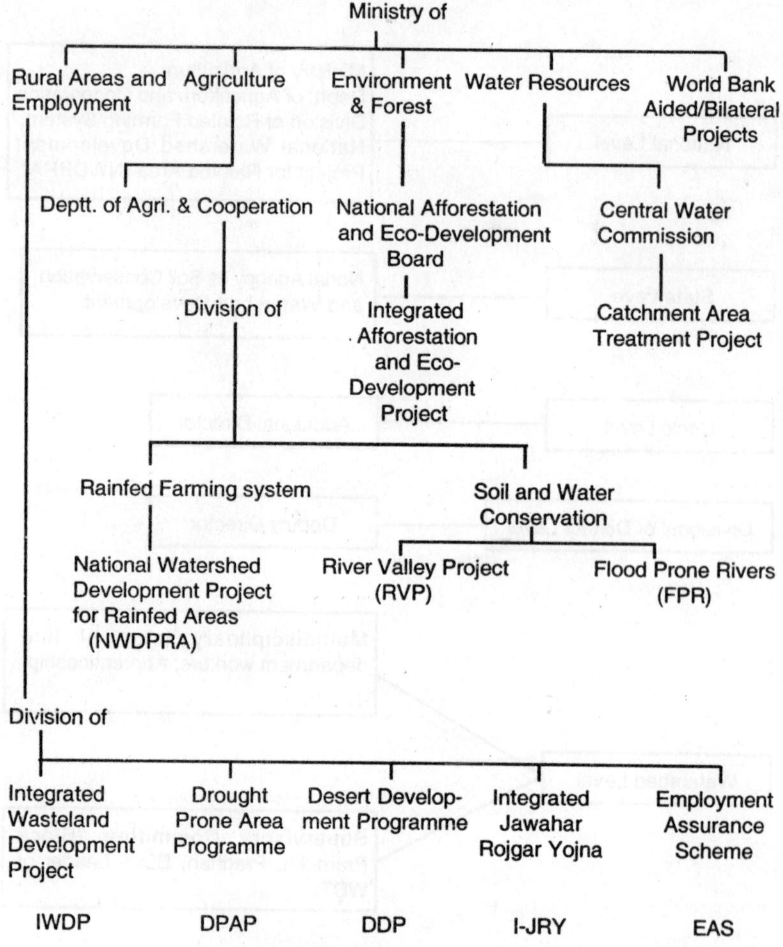

Fig. 4.2 : Watershed Approach and Programmes

in the Rajasthan State. Divisions were further divided into units and Assistant Agricultural Officer (AAO) or Assistant Agricultural Engineer (Asst. Engg.) was head of each unit. These units were further divided into different watersheds and at watershed level, Junior Engineer (Jr. Engg.), a supervisor and an apprentice were appointed. At village level, provision was made for selection of five *mitra kisans* and Self Help Thrift Group (SHTG). These *mitra kisans* would act as contact persons between project staff and farmers.

Functioning of the Project

A series of workshops were organized in August-September 1990 throughout the country to refine and chisel the strategy of implementation of project for Eighth Five Year Plan. The project functioning was decided through organizational system as described previously. Project had not recruited any permanent staff for the purpose and completely depended upon available infrastructure of State and Central government. The soil and water conservation department was mainly responsible to implement the programme at State level. Being a multidisciplinary project, it assumed the involvement of expertise available at district level with Forest, Horticulture, Animal Husbandry, Sericulture, Bee-keeping and small industries departments. The project operates either through Village Panchayat or promoted development of specific organization (informal groups). To do so, the concept of *Mitra Kisan* was advocated. From each village of watershed, five such *Kisans* were to be selected. Out of them, two were woman farmers, two landless farmers (one is called as Gopal to look after animal husbandry) and fifth farmer was from progressive farmers category. The group of *Mitra Kisans* from each village of watershed was known as *Mitra Kisan Mandal* (*MKM*). From each *MKM*, one chairman and a secretary were selected through consensus for a period of one year. Subsequently the secretary is promoted as chairman and another secretary is selected from *MKM*. In this way, a good strength of about fifteen (15) experienced people was planned to be developed during the project period, who could take care of the project after withdrawal. Participation of farmers in survey, planning and preparation, implementation and follow up activities were essential to accelerate the implementation process. Self-Help Thrift Group (SHTG) was to be developed among women farmers and *Mitra Kisans* train to members of SHTG. *Mitra Kisan* helps as change agent in awareness generation, coordination of activities, resolving the conflicts etc. for effective implementation.

Voluntary organization, wherever available would actively be involved in the project for awareness generation, training, nursery raising, monitoring and evaluation. Training for the members of watershed team and *Mitra Kisans* would be imparted at district level. Training manual with details of training strategy and curriculum was developed for the purpose. The training facilities available with ICAR institutes/ SAUs and its centres/KVKs/FTCs/district training centre etc. are to be used for the purpose. Post Graduate in agriculture was appointed as apprentice trainee to each micro-watershed for one year who will work with watershed development team and be paid Rs. 2,500 as stipend per month. In the process, apprentice trainee will be exposed to ground realities of the village problems and will help in quarterly reporting of project.

Observations of Policy Makers at National Level

The project functioning of watershed at national level was analyzed. The information received and observations collected from policy-makers at national level were analyzed and presented as under :

(i) The watershed approach for integrated area development followed in several ministries (Fig.4.2) lacked coordination in sharing problems and experiences.

(ii) At national level, NWDPRA personnel were aware of field reality of project but being in government service they hesitated and did not want to disclose/ share the actual facts. They perceived that without sincere efforts of implementing agency at field level, programme objectives could not be achieved. The effort at field level was not in tune with the NWDPRA objectives.

(iii) Project staff at national level was found over-confident to guidelines prepared for implementation in the form of booklets in the name of WARSA.

(iv) They believed that Joint Secretary (Agriculture), Government of India, was the man behind the programme and after his retirement, programme had not been in the priority.

(v) The guidelines of project circulated at the beginning were modified as per feedback received from fields. It showed that enough groundwork was not done before the start of project. There was mismatch in the project proposal and the ground reality. The implementation procedure was copied simply with some modifications from other rural development agencies.

(vi) The aspect of people's participation was well highlighted, but techniques of participatory development had no place in the guidelines. The assumption might be that people's participation would be the responsibility of State department.

(vii) In general, the perception of personnel from other similar agencies was better for NWDPRA programme when they saw in terms of their own programme.

(viii) The reporting system such as NIC-NET as previously thought for timely monitoring had been found collapsed.

(ix) The State level review of projects was available only in brief and, therefore, much could not be drawn from it.

(x) They had conviction that the programme would continue in coming Five Year Plan.

Features of Selected Watershed

The selected watershed named as Bara Padampura situated

in Block Chaksu of Jaipur district in Rajasthan. It was 35 km. from Jaipur on Jaipur-Tonk road. The watershed comes in the category of (Table 4.1) low productivity and poor investment capacity of farmers. The project received a sum of Rs. 2.34 crore; out of which Rs. 90 lakh could not be spent and was sent back to Central Government.

Table 4.1 : Features of a Selected Watershed

Sl. No.	*Characteristics of watershed*	*Area (ha)*
1.	Total geographical area	6310.70
2.	Arable land	5448.11 (86.33 %)
	(i) Irrigated	587.74 (09.31 %)
	(ii) Unirrigated	4860.37 (77.00 %)
3.	Non-arable land	862.59 (13.66 %)
	(i) Panchayat and pasture land	471.55 (07.47 %)
	(ii) Government land (road, rail side land etc.)	175.44 (02.78 %)
	(iii) Area not available for development (habitation, records, river, mines, lakes etc.)	215.60 (03.42 %)
	(iv) Forest land	Nil
4.	Land available for treatment	6310.70
	(i) Arable	647.00 (10.25 %)
	(ii) Non-arable	5448.11 (86.96 %)

The total geographical area of watershed was 6310.70 ha where non-arable land was 862.59 and arable was 5448.59 ha Non-arable land was divided into Panchayat and Pasture land, government land and area not available for development were 471.56, 175.44 and 215.70 ha respectively. The non-arable cultivable irrigated land was 587.74 and unirrigated land was 4860.37 ha. The land available for treatment was 647.00 ha and arable land was 5488.00 ha.

The total population of watershed was 27,898 living in about 36 villages. The ratio of female was more than male in the watershed and, youths and adults were maximum 16,566 (59.38%) in total population. The selected 6 villages (Table 4.2) of micro watershed did not have forest land. Panchayat land was available in all villages except Yarlipura. The village Barkhera had maximum panchayat land (78.82 ha). Irrigated area was less than unirrigated in all the villages. Shivdaspura village had the maximum land (715.29 ha).

Table 4.2 : Land use Pattern of Selected Villages

Name of villages	*Forest land*	*Panchayat land (ha)*	*Revenue land (ha)*	*Other habitat*	*Irrigated land (ha)*	*Unirrigated land (ha)*	*Total land (ha)*
Dahar	Nil	19.10	05.90	06.26	20.02	203.05	254.33
Saligram-pura	Nil	15.77	07.28	02.49	52.79	186.77	265.10
Barkhera	Nil	78.82	12.09	18.25	91.04	361.62	561.82
Shivdaspura	Nil	46.88	00.64	27.26	65.00	575.41	715.29
Yarlipura	Nil	—	00.21	00.29	06.00	061.55	068.05
Raipuria	Nil	38.61	03.03	03.69	23.80	152.02	221.15
Bilwa	Nil	28.16	03.00	28.45	53.50	486.19	599.30

About 2,208 ha (40.52 %) of total arable land, 5,448.11 ha were sown under *kharif* crops, whereas 2,858 ha (52.45 %) were sown under *rabi* crops. In the *kharif*, bajra was the major crop and recommended varieties of bajra were grown by majority of the farmers. In addition, they used to grow the local varieties of moong and linseed in small area. In *rabi* season, chickpea occupied the maximum area next to wheat.

Among the cattle population, sheep 7,764 (51%) and goat 3,312 (21.4 %) together occupied 72.74 per cent of total cattle population. The cow and buffalo were found with big farmers where sheep and goat with poor farmers.

Land capability classification shows that the maximum (72.47 %) land was in Category I and II together. The land in these two categories was treated as productive and free from problems. As the categories increased, the severity of land problem also increased. The category between III to VI consisted 1626.70 ha (19.71 %) land. There was no land in the last two categories of VII and VIII. Land slope percentage varied from 1 to 8 in selected watershed. Maximum area 4,016 (63 %) was under 1-4 per cent slope.

The rainfall pattern of decade (1980-89) showed maximum rainy days 25 and minimum 14, and the average was 19 in a year. The total rainfall varied from 244.4 to 641.2 mm, with average 433.58 mm per annum. The peak period of rainfall was from 12th July to 22nd August. Temperature varied between 47° C in summer and 20° C during the winter season.

Progress of Work in Selected Watershed

The functional progress of work between 1991 to 1995 was analyzed and consolidated progress report (Table 4.3). The concentration of efforts in project was towards improvement in drainage line of 20 ha existing in the micro-watershed. The width of drainage line was about 100 m, the line developed in 1982 rains. Initially, the line was narrow one. Gradually, it expanded and created havoc to nearby villages.

A total of 22 km Ipomea (*Ipomea carnea*) was planted (for bank stabilization) along drainage line. To treat different Nala's opening in drainage line, 13 live check dams and 29 brush wood dams and 15 loose stone check dams (LSCD) were constructed. A total of 47 earthen strips with vegetative support and 37 dugout ponds were made.

Table 4.3 : Achievements of Watershed Project during 1991 to 1995

Sl. No.	*Activities of the watershed project*	*Achievements*
1.	Ipomea *(Ipomea Carnea)* plantation for bank stabilisation	22 km
2.	Live check dams	13
3.	Brush wood dams	29
4.	Loose stone check dam (LSCD)	15
5.	Earthen stripes with vegetative support	47
6.	Dugout pond	37
7.	Fodder demonstrations	125
8.	Chaffcutter machines	15
9.	Biomass producing units for employment	42
10.	Employment through household component	30
11.	Munja *(Saccharam Munja)* plantation for CVH (arable land)	3300 ha
12.	Single crop demonstrations	647
13.	Inter-crop demonstrations	150
14.	Plantations under agroforestry	70,000
15.	Plantation in undryland horticulture	30,000
16.	Overseeding of grasses, planting trees and shrubs	111 ha
17.	Plantation in pasture land	65,000
18.	User's committee members	53
19.	Members of *mitra kisan mandals*	55

Total of 125 fodder demonstrations were laid out on farmer's field and 15 chaffcutter machines were provided to the farmers on subsidy. Besides these 42 biomass producing units were developed to generate the employment and 30 service sector schemes were arranged for employment in household component of project.

Contour Vegetative Hedge (CVH) through Munja (Saccharam munja) plantation was done in 3,300 ha in arable land and total 647 single crop demonstrations and 150 inter-crop demonstrations were laid out under the project. For these demonstrations, high yielding variety seeds were made available to farmers.

Under the component of arid horticulture, hardy multipurpose trees species were supplied and 70,000 plants under agro-forestry were planted. In dryland horticulture 30,000 plants procured from forest department as well as from nurseries were planted and maintained under watershed project.

The conservation measures used on the non-arable land were vegetative fencing, CVH and gully control. In production component 111 ha of land was used for over-seeding of grasses, planting trees and shrubs etc. Total 65,000 plants were planted in pits at the pasture land.

From the above elaboration it can be said that the work carried out was related to :

(i) Soil conservation with less emphasis on vegetative support.
(ii) Plantation of trees under horticulture and agroforestry.
(iii) Development of plant nurseries.

2. Awareness of Farmers about Watershed Project and its Activities

Sources of Awareness to Farmers

The information on how the beneficiaries came to know about watershed programme was analyzed and presented in (Table 4. 4). The *mitra kisans* who were also working as contractors were the major source of awareness generation as reported by 53.33 per cent farmers. They (*mitra kisan*) mostly told to the farmers about the programme of watershed. Panchayat members and progressive farmers had only 23.33 and 10.00 per cent of share as source of awareness. Mass media and other personnel of government had no role in awareness generation among farmers about the programme.

Table 4.4 : Awareness of Farmers about Watershed Development Project

N=30

Sl. No.	*Sources of awareness*	*No. of farmers*	*Percentage*	*Rank*
1.	*Mitra Kisan* (contractor or mate)	16	53.33	I
2.	Panchayat member	07	23.33	II
3.	Project personnel	03	10.00	IV
4.	Progressive farmers	04	13.34	III
5.	Other personnel of State department	nil	—	—
6.	Mass media	nil	—	—
	Total	30	100	

Awareness about Conservation Measures and Pasture Development

Awareness about watershed activities as observed were categorized in four components i.e. conservation measures, pasture development, crop production and animal husbandry (Tables 4.5 and 4.6). The data showed that the awareness among farming community about the project was maximum for soil conservation followed by pasture development, crop production and animal husbandry component, respectively. The maximum awareness was for conservation activities, whereas the minimum was for cattle development work. Among conservation measures the maximum number of farmers 60 per cent were aware of bunding measures. Vegetative measures like munja (*Saccharam munja*) transplantation 40 per cent, ipomea (*Ipomea carnea*) transplantation 33.33 per cent and ponds making

Table 4.5 : Awareness to Farmers about Soil Conservation and Pasture Development

N=30

Sl. No.	*Awareness for watershed activities*	*No. of farmers*	*Percentage*
I.	**Soil Conservation Measures**		
1.	Bunding on arable land	18	60.00
2.	Munja (*Saccharam munja*) transplantation	12	40.00
3.	Ipomea (*Ipomea carnea*) transplantation for bank stabilization	10	33.33
4.	Ponds making to harvest rain water	08	26.66
5.	Repairing of old ponds	04	13.33
6.	Gully plug to control erosion	03	10.00
7.	Check dam to control erosion	03	10.00
8.	Filter tank	02	06.66
II.	**Pasture Development Component**		
1.	Tree plantation on pasture land	12	40.00
	(i) Digging of pits	10	33.33
	(ii) Subabul (*Leucaena leucocephala*) plantation	03	10.00
	(iii) Ber (*Zizufos zuzube*) plantation	03	10.00
2.	Contour vegetative hedge (CVH) for protection	10	33.33
3.	V-ditch for protection	06	20.00

26.66 per cent were the other activities of awareness for members. Gully plug, check dam, repairing of old ponds were known to few people. Very few farmers were aware of filter tank under well improvement scheme.

The awareness of plantation on pasture land was observed in 40 per cent farmers of the area, digging of pits and contour vegetative hedge 33.33 per cent each. The awareness was very low in making V ditch 20 per cent and plantation of ber (*Zizufos zuzube*) as well as subabul (*Leucaena leucocephala*) 10 per cent in each under the project.

Awareness of Crop Production and Animal Husbandry

The data on awareness about crop production and animal husbandry component of watershed were analysed and presented in Table 4.6. It revealed that as many as 40 per cent of farmers were aware of improved seed distribution programme followed by 26.66 per cent of farmers were aware of distribution of Di-Ammonium Phosphate (DAP). About 20 per cent of farmers had awareness in distribution of Urea fertilizer as well as compost pit making activities. Hardly 16.66 per cent of them were aware of distribution of sprayers and dusters.

Table 4.6 : Awareness of Farmers about Crop Production and Animal Husbandry

N=30

Sl. No.	*Awareness for watershed activities*	*No. of farmers*	*Percentage*
I.	**Crop Production Component**		
1.	Distribution of improved seeds	12	40.00
2.	Distribution of Di-Ammonium Phosphate (DAP)	08	26.66
3.	Distribution of Urea fertilizer	06	20.00
4.	Making compost pits	06	20.00
5.	Distribution of sprayers and dusters	05	16.66
II.	**Animal Husbandry Component**		
1.	Cattle fair in villages	16	53.33
2.	Chaffcutter machines distribution	08	26.66
3.	*Gopal* working for cattle improvement programme	04	13.33
4.	Artificial insemination (A.I.) work	03	10.00
5.	Castration of scared cattle	03	10.00

In case of animal husbandry programme, maximum 53.33 per cent awareness was observed in cattle fair, followed by chaffcutter distribution 26.66 per cent, *Gopal* working for cattle programme 13.33 per cent, artificial insemination and castration programme 10 per cent each.

Awareness of the programme is very first stage of people's participation. The overall awareness of programme was observed to be very low. Farmers were thinking that "Government people are doing some work in and around the villages". It means farmers were aware to only few activities of the project in a disintegrated way. They had a deteriorated picture of the watershed approach as one policy makers says that "at initiation stage the watershed concept had hundred per cent value and at execution only 15 per cent". This indicates that the programme did not involve people and was running on contract basis. Even though the farmers were aware about the part and parcel of the programme. Consequently, the very purpose of involving people was defeated.

3. Organizational, Technological and Socio-economic Issues in Implementation of Project

3.1 Organizational Issues at Field Level

The organizational issues related to watershed development project were studied through direct observations and discussions with respondents individually and in groups. It was observed that organizational issues were inter-related with field activities of watershed. The information so far gathered were presented in Table 4.7.

These informations indicate that there were 10 important issues, which influenced the overall functioning of watershed project. The first issue was that the people working as contractors were selected as *mitra kisans* / contact farmers. The second major issue was about the expectations created in the beginning at farmers meetings, which gave rise to wrong message about the programme in the society. Conflicts between *mitra kisans* and project staff especially on payment observed as third major issues as reported by 47 per cent of respondents. The study revealed that at the time of selection of *mitra kisans*, democratic process was ignored and personal relations dominated. The rich farmers had developed good

Table 4.7 : Organizational Issues at Field Level

N=30

Sl. No.	*Organizational issues*	*No. of Respondents*	*Rank and percentage*
1.	Contractor became *mitra kisans*	20 (66.66 %)	I
2.	Unrealistic expectations created in meetings	15 (50.00 %)	II
3.	Conflicts between project staff and *mitra kisans* over wage payment	14 (46.66 %)	III
4.	Emphasis on personal relations in selection of *mitra kisans*	13 (43.33 %)	IV
5.	Rich farmers had contract works by developing rapport with project personnel	10 (33.33 %)	V
6.	Improper training,work facilities and faith in staff	06 (20.00%)	VI
7.	Involving people means inviting trouble–a team leader's perception	05 (16.66 %)	VII
8.	Duplication of efforts at village level	04 (13.33 %)	VIII
9.	Involvement of city-based migrated people for their own village development	03 (10.00%)	IX
10.	Poor leadership qualities in village people	03 (10.00%)	IX
	Total	93	

rapport with project personnel and succeeded to take some work in watershed project as contractors and not as beneficiaries. There was no proper training for the *mitra kisans* and work facilities were poor. The perception of *mitra kisans* differed on people's participation. Few local leaders also thought that involving people was "inviting trouble". The rich farmers were largely taking benefits of the programme.

The animal husbandry component was not successful due to lack of proper training of *mitra kisans* and lack of veterinary facilities at field level. Duplication of efforts was also observed in different activities at village level that created confusion among villagers about the jurisdiction of different agencies working for the same cause. It was also observed that involvement of city based educated migrated people can be an asset for their respective villages in mobilizing people. These people may be more helpful in the selection of actual *mitra kisans* having support of local people.

It is apparent from the above that in implementation of watershed projects, the prescribed guidelines were ignored and poor effort was made to involve common people in the programme.

Emphasis on Personal Relation in Selection of Mitra Kisan

Mr. Ruplal Sharma an agriculture supervisor in watershed project first visited to Sh. Ramesh Jain, a young farmer of a small village, close to Bara Padampura (Padampura) town. Sh. Ruplal Sharma was a good friend of Ramesh Jain; told him that he wanted to begin some work like bunding and digging of ponds etc. under watershed project. A group of *mitra kisans* from each village of micro-watershed was required at watershed level for functioning of project. After that, about 10 persons (one or two from few villages) were chosen orally on spot as *mitra kisan* and Ramesh Jain himself declared as chairman of *mitra kisan mandal*. Thus, a committee of *mitra kisans* was constituted at watershed level. The activities of project were started under the supervision of Shri Ramesh and other known members of selected *mitra kisan mandal*. As a friend Mr. Sharma was free to share all sorts of views with Shri Ramesh. Here, Sharma was giving direction only to Shri Ramesh. Other members of *mitra kisan mandal* were never involved. During visits, most of the discussions on watershed activities between Sharma and Ramesh were held at a shop of Padampura town and major decisions were taken at this place.

It was observed that implementation of the project was in *ad hoc* manner and in hurry without constituting the committees. The panchayat and others views were not considered at all. The close associates were allowed for benefits. Only major activities of project were started at beginning. The supervisor did not disclose the programme in public knowingly.

Involving People means inviting Trouble—*A Team Leader's Perception*

Shri Ramesh Jain viewed that at the beginning, good work

was done because of few people had knowledge about the programme and decision making was centered in a few hands. As the time passed, people of nearby villages came to know through farmer to farmer communication about the project. As a result, other local people made a strong protest as to why "they were" not involved in the programme and "how" Ramesh and his men (close associates) were taking benefits from government scheme. With these developments, few local people of area came forward to take some cash/ kind benefits and "*netagiri*" was started in scheme as reported by Ramesh. Thus, the power of decision making was marginalised from Shri Ramesh. Local leaders had started questioning the supervisor whenever he visited the field to know the details of the project. Few *mitra kisans* felt that there should not be any more propaganda about the programme as it would create problem for them.

The wrong perception of *mitra kisans* was due to their personal motives. They did not like the advantages taken by them, should be shared among the people. The observation concludes that decision making was centered in few hands at the beginning. For implementing of the programme awareness was not thoroughly generated so that each one could not be involved to decide upon right course of action.

Rich Farmers Developed Rapport with Project Personnel

About twenty local leaders made their efforts to collect information about watershed project. These people had good contact to urban area and their socio-economic status was high. They visited very frequently to head office of watershed development project located at Jaipur. With their frequent visits project staff had developed a feeling of insecurity from these local people. They critically tried to know the programme of watershed and the role of local people. A few of them developed regular contact and won confidence of the project staff like Junior Engineer (Jr. Engg.) and Supervisor. Few of them finally succeeded in getting some work. These local people had no cooperation among themselves so they approached project personnel independently and persuaded to staff in their own way.

The rich people having good linkage to urban area, were front-runners in programme implementation. Initially staff had fear in mind from these people and consequently decided to implement the activities through them.

Contractor became Mitra Kisan

The local leader in fact were the contractors locally called *mate*. In those villages where the contractors were not available; new members were selected as *mitra kisans*. These *mates* made their presence in project by sharing some activities from Ramesh. The important role of these contractors was observed in field as managing the labour from outside or within watershed area to complete the targets. It was found that about 30 migrated labourer of Haryana had worked under the project for 2-3 months in a year. These people stayed in school premises and were taken care by the contractors. Assistant engineer (Asst. Engg.) of project helped to arrange these labours. On the other side many people of watershed were migrating in search of job to urban areas like Jaipur where they were earning good wages (Rs. 64 per day) while in the watershed project the provision was Rs. 33 per day.

How the relationship develop between *mitra kisans* and project staff and why contractors system was introduced? — were the issue emphasizing the need of training of the implementing agencies on participatory approach.

The result concludes that *mitra kisans* were not properly selected and contractors were treated as *mitra kisans*. They were working for personal motives and there was no concern for observing the procedure and involving all in the programme. Local people were not educated about the programme and most of them used to work in other places to get higher wages.

Unrealistic Expectations created in Meetings

After detailed case analysis, it was found that in first meeting with farmers the approach followed by project staff to generate awareness was improper. Such a meeting continued for 3 hours in Saligrampura but participants could not get the project. The project staff said, "give us time we will change the fortune". They were assured to be helped by giving the cow, buffalo, goat, bull, sheep, poultry, medicines for cattle, duster and spray machines, hybrid seeds etc., in addition to training in pickles and mat making. They were asked to fill up application forms in the meetings itself. Promises were also made to give loan on poultry as well as on agricultural machines, and also Rs. 1,000 as subsidy under few activities of programme. These promises created an image in people that they would get direct benefit either in cash or kind from the project. They had been waiting since the beginning to fulfil such motives from project.

Thus the approach for awareness generation was not proper and might be due to ignorance in project staff on implementation process as well as goal of project or very hurry for the completion of targets. In this way instead of creating proper awareness about project, unrealistic expectations were created in meetings. These had acted adversely and the people lost faith in the programme when their expectations were not fulfilled.

Conflicts between Project Staff and Mitra Kisan over Wage Payment

The labourer worked in watershed projects were not paid for more than one year. Contractors blamed to office for delay. The labour met the contractors daily for their payments. Provisionally, the payment to labourers was to be made on structural measurement, but labourer wanted it on the basis of per labour per day. Sometimes wrong measurement of structures as well as manipulation in attendance of the labourer working for the watershed activities also created problems. The project personnel argued that the contractors were usually showing wrong attendance of labourer, so payment should be based on measurement of structure. This created a conflict among labourer, contractors and project staff, and ultimately affected the implementation process of watershed.

Further the labourer of the project area did not have feeling that this was their programme. They had only concern for their wages for work as observed. These observations reveal that participatory process was almost lacking and only consideration was to fulfil the project target by any means.

Improper Training, Work Facilities and Faith in Staff

Mr. Tejkaran, a farmer of Shivdaspura came to know about training of cattle development and requirement of *mitra kisan*. He was told that the selected person had to undergo four months training at Jaipur and during this period Rs. 20 per day would be given as honorarium. Tejkaran was not convinced at the beginning. Jr. Engg. Mr. Dhariwal, tried to convince him and made him agree for participation in the programme. When Tejkaran was under training, Mr. Dhariwal was transferred from Jaipur. Tejkaran came back without completing the training course. He thought that without Mr. Dhariwal he could not do the job successfully. Supervisor Mr. Sharma persuaded Tejkaran to go back for training. However, without completing training course, somehow he got certificate for working as *gopal* (*mitra kisan*) under the project. He was not doing what he had learned in training. Once Mr. Dhariwal came on an unofficial visit and asked him to do the job, otherwise their official would blame Dhariwal that, why selection was made for such a person. Thus, Tejkaran decided to do whatever possible but he was facing a number of problems due to poor work facilities at village level.

The results conclude that faith of local people in the project staff had its own value. Selection of person for training whether he is able to take responsibility was very important.

Duplication of Efforts at Village Levels

Three government agencies i.e. DRDA, forest and watershed department and four non government organizations were working in the same watershed area. Though their goals were different, but everybody wanted to get people's participation. Each agency was trying to formulate group/society at village level and the members of these groups were more or less same, who used to participate at village level meetings. The situation had created a doubt among village people that which agency wanted to do what? There was no coordination among these agencies at village level. Due to several agencies, sometimes senior government officials were misguided and were shown the work done by other agencies on their field visits.

Based on these observations the study suggests that at village level an appropriate plan needs to be prepared by the village people. The development agencies should act as facilitator. The activities of different agencies should be spelt out and better coordination of agencies should be ensured at village level to avoid duplication of efforts.

3.1.1. Organizational Issues related to Implementing Agency

The organizational issues concerned to implementing agency were analyzed and presented in Table 4.8.

It showed that certain policy issues affected the implementation drastically. The delay in payment was observed due to complex procedure and wrong policy of fund flow system. There were few good workers in the staff but due to frequent transfer, the programme had to suffer, especially the faith of farmers in the project was lost. The organizational values deteriorated fast. Poor coordination in multi-disciplinary team due to incorrect policy and unavailability of transport was also observed. The planning was not according to farmer's need and it depended on

Table 4.8 : Organizational Issues at Agency Level

N=30

Sl. No.	*Organizational issues*	*No. of Respondents and percentage*	*Rank*
1.	Complex procedure and guidelines of funding	22 (73.33 %)	I
2.	Frequent transfer affects rapport building	18 (60.00 %)	II
3.	Deterioration in organizational climate	17 (56.66 %)	III
4.	Only few good workers in staff	14 (46.66 %)	IV
5.	Poor coordination in departments	11 (36.66 %)	V
6.	Lack of basic data for planning	10 (33.33 %)	VI
7.	On the spot planning	08 (26.66 %)	VII
8.	More dependency on field staff	06 (20.00 %)	VIII
9.	Lack of facilities for night stay in field	03 (10.00 %)	IX
	Total	109	

availability of funds in programmes. At the beginning of the project, proper survey was not carried out and the informations collected from secondary sources were not fully updated since long. Due to poor supervision, field staff chalked out the plan on their own that proved to be wrong and lot of money was wasted in this way. More dependence on field level staff was observed and that caused loss of the initiative for work.

Lack of Basic Data for Planning

Bara Padampura watershed was selected in 1991. Benchmark survey, which was a prerequisite, was not done according to guidelines of the project. The necessary information for planning was collected from secondary sources were outdated, as the respective State department officials did not update these informations since long time. The activities of project were planned on the basis of these informations whereas the actual field condition was different. This was noticed at the time of implementation of the project activities. The Deputy Director of the watershed project was also reluctant to benchmark survey. As a result, the rest of staff took it casually. They perceived it as tedious job.

Complex Procedure for Funding

The procedure for payment to labour was complex and rules at national level were changed very frequently in this respect. The project guidelines suggests that leader of watershed development team would be the final authority to take decision on expenditure of money. But State government changed the system. Initially. authority for passing the bill was with Junior Engineer (Jr. Engg.) which was later shifted to Assistant Engineer (Asst. Engg.). Funds were not released from government in time at watershed level. Joint bank account between Jr. Engg. and chairman of MKM, producing bill and submission to treasury and payment by cheque made the procedure further more complicated. Monthly payment that was being made in first week for some time was also changed subsequently.

Trial and error method in fund flow was observed from government side and the procedure finally adopted was more complex and caused delay in wage payment.

Frequent Transfer affects Rapport Building

Mr. Baldeo Choudhary, a Jr. Engg., was posted in Command Area Development Project and was attached to collector office in Udaipur. He was interested to come to Jaipur. He approached for transfer through political channel and succeeded in March 1995 to get posted in the watershed department since he had experience of a training programme of watershed development. Mr. Dhariwal was already working at Jaipur since his first posting and was associated with the project from beginning. The staff and people of watershed area were impressed with the attitude and work of Mr. Dhariwal. Mr. Choudhary replaced Mr. Dhariwal from Jaipur to Sawaimadhopur. In this process, the rapport building at field level was affected negatively. The farmers had already developed their faith in Dhariwal and when he was transferred, they became inactive and changed their attitude towards the project activities. Dhariwal was also unhappy with those developments.

The observation suggests that there was frequent transfer of project staff, which was not desirable. The transfer policy of government affected the faith of farmers and attitude of project staff negatively. Once a staff creates a climate for change at grass root level, he should not be transferred, rather should be rewarded for his good work. The transfer policy should be appropriate. This would help in building confidence in both project staff and the village people.

Only Few Good Worker in Staff

Several farmers perceived that Jr. Engg. Dhariwal had never encouraged disputes among the *mitra kisans* but, they found Ramesh Jain and Choudhary involved in such act. Dhariwal was brilliant, laborious and sincere worker. It was observed that sometimes he spent more than 12 hours at the site to supervise the work. The farmers informed that he used to stay at night among the village people for rapport building. "His behaviour influenced me and Dhariwal was a nice person" said by Mr. Tejkaran, working as *gopal*. It was also reported that Dhariwal used to conduct fortnightly meeting of farmers, whereas Mr. Choudhary did not follow the practice and he was also misguided by the supervisor Mr. Sharma. Moreover new Jr. Engg. was not frequent visitor to project area. As a result, the farmers became indifferent to project staff and lost confidence in the staff and programme. They opined "when project staff do not participate in the programme, how can they ask farmers to do so".

It means good behaviour, friendly approach, honesty, sincerity for work, team spirit, knowledge of work, hard work, more time with farmers for encouraging harmony in village people, frequent meetings with farmers were the characteristics required to win the faith of village people by staff members. These characteristics affected the implementation in their own way.

Poor Coordination and Transport Facilities

When asked for the reactions about farmers complaints to Jr. Engg. Mr. Choudhary said, "he was not regular visitor to field", Jr. Engg. reacted that besides going to watershed area he had other important duties such as visits to *Tahsildar* and *Patwari,* who were not cooperative. He told that developing pastureland under plantation, requires legal sanction from revenue department and, therefore, he had visited them frequently. In case of manpower and transport at watershed level, Mr. Choudhary said, "Thirty villages are hanging on my neck. Without vehicle it is not possible to look after such a big watershed ". He said, "at least provision of a motorcycle must be made in the project". The jeep of the office was not in function for a long time. Provision of coordination from other line departments was in guidelines and the letters were issued to these departments from time to time, but nobody could turn up for attending the meetings. The common perception in multidisciplinary work was that "watershed project is the programme of soil and water conservation department and all credit will go to that agency/staff caused poor coordination from line departments."

These observations concludes that frustration in staff was also due to poor support from concerned department and lack of transport facilities. The catchment was large in size. The tendency who or which agency would get credit of project was dominated. As a result, the project received poor coordination of different agencies for work.

Dependence on Subordinate Staff

A Deputy Director (DD) in a field visit desired to see the spot where current work was going on under the project. It was observed that Jr. Engg. Mr. Choudhary had knowledge of work, that somewhere digging of a pond (dugout pond) was going on, but he was not aware of the actual location, as he never visited that spot. His supervisor had taken all the decisions about the location and size of the dugout pond. However, supervisor directed the team to reach the site. In the discussion at the site where work of dugout pond was in progress through a tractor, Mr. Choudhary to oblige the DD said "Sir, this is the desilting tank". But the structure was technically known as "dugout pond". This was a shocking statement to DD and finally, he clarified difference between the two to Mr. Choudhary.

This shows that the senior staff was more dependent on field level staff who was not technically sound but involved in taking several important decisions at field level.

On the Spot Planning — A Site Observation

Once said by an ADG of ICAR that the yardstick of work in government system is "expenditure of money". The following incidence of planning and expenditure observed in the study aimfully proved this statement.

Team I : A team led by agriculture supervisor along with five *mitra kisans* walked about 5 km to observe the situation in drainage line. The purpose behind the visit was to re-start the work under the project that was postponed since last six months due to poor health of Jr. Engg. Mr Choudhary. The month was December 1995 and by March 1996, Rs. 25 lakh was to be spent due to closing of the year. During the site observation by the team, in about one and a half hour, a total of Rs. one lakh had been decided to spend on constructing six (6) earthen check dams on the bank of drainage line by March 1996. The team members were not sure that how much catchment area a particular check dam would cover. Thus, to gear up the work, all discussions for planning happened in hurriedly on the way on tractor was running at site without much consideration of the technical requirements.

Team II : After two weeks of the first visit, another team of watershed project consisting a Deputy Director, two Asst. Engg. and one Jr. Engg. assisted by agriculture supervisor and few *mitra kisans* visited the same site where first team already took some decisions to spend Rs. one lakh. This team not only changed the place, height and width of check dams but also suggested for incorporating vegetative barriers along with few check dams. Team members also visualized and considered catchment area for total runoff to be drained to particular structure.

In this way, all the decisions of the Team-I were cancelled and planning done by Team-I could not be implemented. Only a visit of responsible authority changed the scenario of plan.

Thus, it was obvious that watershed development projects involved casual way of planning, planning without considering actual facts and planning by inexperienced hand. In practice "money decided the plan; not the plan decided the money" to solve the problems.

Deterioration in Organizational Climate

An informal discussion of 10 ADMs (Assistant District Magistrate) revealed that Block Development Officers (BDOs) were not cooperative to their officers. Each BDO had developed link with politicians. A few years ago, the situation was not like that. The officials felt that time might come when BDOs would never reach to listen the ADMs in their offices. It was also observed that after office hours, staff members used the offices for enjoying liquor.

These observations suggest that there is bureaucracy in the system and lack of congenial climate in the organization.

3.2. Technological Issues in Project Implementation

The technological issues of watershed projects were analysed using different methods. The gathered informations were presented in Table 4.9.

Table 4.9 : Technological Issues in Implementation of Watershed Project

N=30

Sl. No.	*Technological issues*	*No. of Respondents and percentage*	*Rank*
1.	Failure of technology, reasons and farmers faith	22 (73.33 %)	I
2.	Use of tractor in place of local labour—a violation of guidelines	16 (53 .33 %)	II
3.	Farmers' suggestions not incorporated by contractors	15 (50.00 %)	III
4.	Wrong intention in acceptance of technology	13 (43.33 %)	IV
5.	Indigenous knowledge had no place	11 (36.66 %)	V
6.	Lack of flexibility due to fixed guidelines	10 (33.33 %)	VI
7.	Concern for immediate and personal benefit	09 (30.00 %)	VII
8.	Target approach to technology acceptance	06 (20.00 %)	VIII
9.	Attitude in adoption of technology	06 (20.00 %)	VIII
10.	Problems in cattle development component	05 (16.66 %)	IX
11.	Farmer's influence on project staff for personal benefits	05 (16.66 %)	IX
12.	The recommendation for technology had differed among agencies	04 (13.33 %)	X
	Total	122	

The results indicate that due to poor management and lack of supervision, appropriate technology did not get through and as a result, farmers lost confidence in technology and ultimately faith in programme. Tractors were used to carry out the work which was to be carried through local labourers. However, the message of guideline was modified to their own benefit and feasibility. There was no discussion on the utilization of technological inputs. It was decided and implemented by *mitra kisans* without considering farmers' suggestions and their cooperation. The farmers' intention of getting cash/kind benefits might be the reason for non-consideration of farmer's suggestions. The farmers in general were found looking for the cash/kind benefit from the project. Further, the farmers were practicing several indigenous technologies which were not taken into account in the programme. The farmers' opinion about acceptance of technology was also found negative in some cases.

Target Approach to Technology Acceptance

When asked for the record of the project activities, the team leader Ramesh avoided to share the information. In fact, there was no proper recording of activities and information. Based on his recall, he told that under the watershed project, the major activities completed were construction of earthen check dam and gully plugs, digging of few ponds, tree plantation in 5.0 ha area, distribution of fertilizers and seeds worth Rs. 60 thousand, fertilizers (20 kg Urea and 20 kg DAP) to each farmer and 10 chaffcutters were given to about 1,000 people including SC and ST category under the project. The proper record was not maintained for all these activities.

The approach was to complete the targets and spend the amount on different activities as decided under the project. The needs and aspirations of farmers were ignored and there was no inter-relationship among adopted technologies.

Concern for Immediate and Personal Benefit

The project involved plantation work on the pasture land to provide fodder and fuel to the farmers. The project staff could not convince the farmers for the same. The farmers had bitter experiences of forest department, which did not allow them for grazing of their cattle in forest area after the plantation. They had this kind of fear in mind and, therefore, did not allow the pasture land for plantation. On the other hand, the technology package in the form of improved seeds and fertilizers was well received by farmers.

The technologies related to deep bore well and installation of pumpsets would have helped the farmers, but project had no such provision because of their high cost. Farmers reported that groundwater in the area was becoming alkaline as a result of high discharge and low *in situ* conservation.

The study suggests that views and opinions of farmers on the technological issues should be given due attention. This demand a bottom up planning approach, which was lacking in the project.

Wrong Intentions in Acceptance of Technology

It was noticed that the pits for making compost were dug under the project by farmers in village Dahar and Saligrampura. This was done to get the benefits of the project i.e. bricks of Rs. 1000, one bag of cement and Rs. 70 as wage for digging in the name of composting. The intentions were to receive these facilities for other purposes. They were not at all interested in compost making and project staff also did not try to motivate the farmers about the benefits. The pits so far dug were never used for composting rather these created problem to cattle at grazing in the area.

Thus, efforts made did not serve any purpose. Farmers were not properly educated about the benefit of technology and farmers' intentions were to receive direct benefit of programme.

Attitude in Adoption of Technology

It was found that few farmers did not want to change the shape of their farm by making bunds, because they thought, it would divide the farm land in many parts. Due to this attitude, many farmers were in dilemma whether to do or not the bunding work in their fields. Some farmers adopted the technology and made bunds on their farms before rainy season, but they did not maintain desired height and as a result, the bunds were washed away during the rains. Finally, these farmers dropped the idea of bund making and they negatively influenced other farmers. The farmers also complained that the work of bunding and *munja* plantation was done over the field of those who gave money to contractors.

Farmers' Suggestions were not incorporated

Sh. J.P. Meena, a farmer of Yarlipura, told that once 3-4 contractors visited with tractors and without consulting him took the soil near the boundary of pond and raised the sidewall of the pond. After some time during rain, the soil was eroded back to the same place. The contractors simply completed contract work and they did not maintain required height for increasing the capacity/volume of pond. The contractors didn't accept any suggestion of farmers and did the work on their own way.

No serious attempt was made for the adoption of appropriate technology. Thus, advocated technologies were partially adopted and their total benefits were not realized. This in turn created problem and developed negative attitude towards the spread of technology.

Use of Tractor in place of Local Labour—Violation of Guidelines

Generating and providing employment to the people of watershed area was the major task of the programme. Observations at the field level showed that agriculture supervisor Mr. Sharma and Chairman of watershed development team were using their own tractors for constructing earthen checkdam, improvement of ponds and transporting grasses under the project. They perceived that the "tractor was more economical than human labour. Frequent movement of tractor on the wall of earthen check-dam would make dam more solid and durable. Early rainy season was the peak period for watershed activities and there was always a dearth of labour and even availability of tractor in this period. So, without using tractor, targets of project could not be completed in time. Hence, most of the work was done by tractor and only where tractor was not possible to reach in the field, labour was used for watershed activities.

The completion of targets forced the field staff to sideline the guidelines. The intention of field level project staff and contractor was also to earn more money.

Failure of Technology and Farmers Faith

Case I

In the field of Hanuman Shahay Sharma during 1992, six gully plugs were constructed to control the runoff through nala and in next rains, all the structures were broken. The project staff said that this time rains were heavy, so structure could not sustain. In second year, Gabian structure was made by the use of wire and stones. Time to time senior officials visited the field, and took a number of photographs. These snaps were circulated to owner of field and neighbours. Third year when Gabian structures were again washed away by stream of water, the farmers reacted sharply and became helpless in this matter. After that, the project staff approached the farmers with another proposal/scheme of digging pond on their fields. The farmers did not accept it.

The technological failure acted negatively and farmers lost faith on the technology and in project staff.

Case II

In order to check the siltation, priority in the project was fixed for 20 hactares drainage line. During the year 1993-94, twenty earthen checkdams of about 5 × 1 sq m were constructed on the bank of drainage line to check the runoff. A high amount of money under conservation component was spent. The construction work was carried out under the supervision of *mitra kisans*. On field observation it was found that more than 80 per cent structures were broken by rainwater. Therefore, an attempt was made to find facts behind these broken structures. The following facts were observed :

(1) Heavy rains just after the construction of checkdam.
(2) When these structures were constructed, at that time catchment area had not been taken into account. How much runoff would be received at each structure, had not been estimated.
(3) At the time of planning they moved from lower to higher altitude to estimate runoff. The team then later realised that to check the runoff they were supposed to move from higher to lower altitude so that total runoff could roughly be estimated and accordingly size of structure was to be decided. This realization came after a lesson of trial and error method used in the project, which caused a loss of huge amount of government/public money.

The reason for these failures were further studied taking individual cases in depth. There were other reasons also. Mr. Mathur, Asst. Engg. told that in this area, the soil was full of concrete granules. After the rains when runoff water gathered on the earthen wall of checkdam, the concrete particles were got separated from the soil and washed away. As a result, during coming rains when runoff water put little force on the wall; the wall of checkdams had broken down. That was a natural reason behind breaking of earthen check dam. Mr. Mathur also explained the difficulty in rectifications in such type of soil and told "it will happen again". The sole solution would be zigzag structures to slow down the runoff force. As in the same area an unbroken earthen checkdam was made which in its catchment had about twenty small zigzag structures were intact.

(6) The old day's practice of sheep penning was popular among the farmers and almost all farmers were following it. Now it is not common and few only were practicing.

(7) The boiled unused tea was used for the treatment of dysentery in sheep. The practice has been adopted by few farmers from several years. Similarly, the swollen throat of sheep is reported to be ameliorated through guar seeds. The logic of farmer was that in the process of juggle, guar seed used to absorb the surplus water from swollen part of throat and help in early recovery.

3.3. Socio-economic Issues

A forest officer reported on people's participation "that 70 per cent farmers are small and marginal in villages. They were never free and always busy in their work. Hardly they had time to participate in the project. About 25 per cent of them were big and they had no interest in the project. Only 5 per cent were those who could help and initiate the programme."

The socio-economic issues related to watershed project were observed from selected respondents and others in-groups. The issues so emerged were recorded and presented in Table 4.10.

Table 4.10 : Socio-economic Issues affecting Implementation of the Project

N=30

Sl. No.	*Socio-economic issues*	*No. of Respondents* and *percentage*	*Rank*
1.	Lack of conflicts resolution system		
	(i) Conflict for common property resources	12 (40.00 %)	IV
	(ii) Conflict over selection of people for training	18 (60.00 %)	II
	(iii) Conflict over sharing benefits	20 (66.66 %)	I
	(iv) Conflict between *mitra kisans* and farmers	10 (33.33 %)	V
2.	Problems in convincing the farmers	06 (20.00 %)	VI
3.	Lack of concern for the development of farmers	15 (50.00 %)	III

After implementation of the project several conflicts emerged among people in villages but due to lack of conflict resolutions mechanism especially through meetings etc. people had a wrong message of the programme. It showed that lack of interaction among society member, improper distribution of inputs, conflict among farmers over sharing of common benefits, low status of women in society were the important issues needed to be resolved. Farmers thinking for development was individualistic and rarely follow group approach.

Lack of Conflicts Resolution System

Case I

The Acasia plantation had been done on small piece of land of about one acre at the beginning of project. The plant leaves were used for cattle feeding particularly the sheep. Once conflict arose over cutting of 13 tender plants by some people from the common land in Saligrampura. Against this issue, few women came forward to take action. Sarpanch of village lodged FIR at police station. Due to this incidence an honest person Mr. Ramkedar resigned from chairmanship of society, when he could not resolve the issue. How to resolve these conflicts in participatory way was a unanswerable question among farmers. Most of the village people were in view that project staff should appoint a watchman in night hours but the people of village did not find any possibility inside the village to manage the situation. In order to manage common property resources, it was felt that women initiative was more appreciative.

Case II

Narmada Devi, a widow of 55 years of village Dahar, had no land and job. Big size of family was a problem to her. She required direct help from the Government. People of village had sympathy to her, so they recommended her name for two days training at Jaipur under watershed programme.

She participated in training programme and received Rs. 40 for a day as honorarium. The moot point was that those attended the training were not the member of society, so member of society should be given preference for training. When Narmada Devi was asked about their learning for training programme, she said "only seen a video film and remembers very little of it". She could not explain the utility of film for village.

Case III

The following are some small issues were observed :

- Rajesh, the chairman (*MKM*) of Saligrampura gave the impression to women members of society that watershed was his own work and he had sole responsibility for decision making. The other society members would get their due benefit at appropriate time.
- Sharda Devi, a member of *MKM* in Saligrampura had never participated and interacted with members and even could not know the name of other members of groups.
- Ramkedar Sharma reported that chairman of village Dahar was only influential person benefited from crop demonstration component of project. Many people did not receive the seed even once. In distribution of maize seed, supervisor said to women farmers that somebody had taken their shares on her name. The chairman Rajesh announced that if one will take mustard, then bajra would not be given to that person. The concept of seed demonstration failed. There was no proper system to discuss and decide with farmers for the programme. As a result everyone was interested in getting the seed in any quantity and this created conflict among the farmers.

It can be concluded from the above mentioned cases that the project staff and *mitra kisans* should be trained to resolve such issues through participatory action i.e. community sanction or fine. The study indicates those selected for the training were not members of the watershed society. The selection of trainees was on sympathetic ground only to get honorarium. The criteria for selection was *ad hoc,* the practical utility of training was not the concern in the selection. As a result, training imparted was unutilized in the project.

Conflict between Mitra Kisan and Farmers

1. The farmers reported that payments for labour were made on incorrect measurement of structures. Incorrect bills were passed, there was no *khasra,* treasury number and signature at time of payment. Bills were made at *chopal* of village without visiting site of actual work. Once the payment had been made in a village school of Saligrampura and the situation became violent. As a result, work at site stopped for long time. A bold lady from village Saligrampura made voice against wrong payments; she made request to authorities of watershed project after getting signature of village people but action was not taken by authorities of watershed. Farmers complained that Aldrin and DAP fertilisers were black-marketed by few chairmen in nearby local market. Chaffcutter machine was supposed to be given at Rs. 950 after subsidy but the same was distributed in Rs. 1100 without any bill and voucher.
2. The major work was done in drainage-line and not on farmers field, so farmers were not happy because drainage line was common property. Farmers were also not ready to contribute money, even few farmers did not allow project staff for work at their field.
3. The problem of encroachment of land was major hurdle in implementing certain activities of project. Owner of farm field, around the pasture had

encroached more than 40 acres of land and in the language of Jr. Engg. Mr. Choudhary, — "Kisano Ne Attyachar Kar Rakha Hai". These farmers were not intended to free the land. Disputes among the member of watershed societies occurred frequently on issue of encroachment.

4. In village Kalkipura a *Barani Chetna Kendra* was developed under the watershed project. The purpose of the Kendra was to maintain the office of project and raise the plant nurseries in the same premises. There was nothing, people had taken away the materials like wooden frame of doors, windows and also bricks used in constructing the Kendra. It was told that the construction was not on appropriate site and usually nobody used to pass from that place. There was no permanent staff of the project who could look after the premises. As few farmers told that the Kendra should be on common place on the way, so that people could easily visit and consult for guidance.
5. It was also observed that shepherds destroyed Gabien structures and they also put fire in brushwood structures during winter to warm up themselves. "This is government programme" was common feeling, so village people destroy some of the work under project.

It can be concluded that corruption, vested interest of society members, lack of sharing and non cooperation influenced people. So farmers had different perception and that perception needs to be changed by persuasion.

Perception/Experiences of Project Personnel on Selected Aspects of Watershed Project

This part of study deals with perception of project personnel on the following aspects presented as :

- Education, experiences, awareness and knowledge,
- Relative importance of watershed components and job involvement,
- Training and its effectiveness,
- Factors in people's participation under the project,
- Education, experiences, awareness and knowledge.

Education, Experiences, Awareness and Knowledge

Educational Level of Project Personnel

The educational level of project personnel showed that they had their education either in agriculture or agricultural engineering (Table 4.11).

Table 4.11 : Educational Level of Project Personnel

N=70

Sl. No.	*Educational level*	*No. of Respondents*	*Percentage*
1.	B.Sc. Ag.	34	48.57
2.	B.Sc. Ag. (Engg.)	13	18.57
3.	M.Sc. Ag.	10	14.28
4.	M.Sc.Ag. (Engg.)	05	07.14
5.	Ph.D	08	11.42
	Total	70	100.00

The majority (more than 67 per cent) of them was from first-two categories i.e. Graduate, whereas about 21 per cent had Master degree and 12 per cent Doctorate degree indicating that the staff was adequately qualified. As it was observed that agriculture engineering graduates had technocratic mentality and was poor in group mobiiization at field level over agriculture background people.

Experience of Project Personnel

The experiences of project personnel (Table 4.12) in watershed development showed that majority of the personnel were having 1 to 15 years of experience. It was also observed that respondents were not very much clear to express their length of experience in watershed development. This may be because they had doubt, that the experience of soil and water conservation and watershed development was similar or different.

Table 4.12 : Experience of Project Personnel in Watershed Development

N=70

Sl. No.	*Years of experience*	*No. of Respondents*	*Percentage*
1.	1–5	15	21.42
2.	5–10	18	25.71
3.	10–15	9	12.85
4.	15–20	5	07.14
5.	20–25	8	11.42
6.	25-30	4	05.71
7.	30–35	7	10.00
8.	35–40	4	05.71
	Total	72	100.00

Awareness about Successful Watershed Projects

An analysis on awareness of the project staff about successful watershed project was made whether they were aware or not. It was observed that as many as 66 per cent project personnel were not aware of any successful watershed project (Table 4.13).

Table 4.13 : Awareness of Project Personnel about Successful Watershed Projects

N=70

Sl. No.	*Awareness to successful watershed projects*	*No. of Respondents*	*Percentage*
1.	Aware	24	34.28
2.	Not aware	46	65.72
	Total	70	100.00

The project personnel (34%) were aware of about 14 successful projects of the State. Only a few of them said they had information of Sukhomanjari and Ralegaon Siddhi projects of watershed development, which are regarded as model watershed projects.

Knowledge of Project Objectives

The project personnel were asked about their knowledge of the objectives of watershed development project (Table 4.14). The analysis of data showed that 85 per cent had correct perception to objectives of watershed development project, whereas only 15 per cent could not respond correctly. The people who responded correctly gave holistic meaning of watershed development and others only part of the watershed development. It means that they had correct perception to objectives of watershed development project.

Table 4.14 : Knowledge of Project Personnel about Objectives of Watershed Development

N=70

Sl. No.	*Response*	*No. of Respondents*	*Percentage*
1.	*Correct*	*60*	*85.71*
2.	*Not correct*	*10*	*14.29*
	Total	*70*	*100.00*

Perception on Relatively Important Programme Activities and Job Involvement of Project Personnel

Perception on Relatively Important Programme Activities

The perception of project personnel on the important activities for success of watershed indicated (Table 4.15) that, resource conservation and production measures were perceived relatively more important than socio-economic and

Table 4.15 : Relative Importance of Activities for Success of Watershed Project as Perceived by Project Personnel

N=70

Sl. No.	*Perceived activities*	*No. of Respondents*	*Percentage*
I.	**Resource Conservation and Production Measures**		
1.	Rain water harvesting and use	23	32.85
2.	Crop/food production	21	30.00
3.	Fodder production	19	27.14
4.	Conservation of soil and water	16	22.85
5.	Judicial use of natural resources	14	20.00
6.	Development of forest	13	18.57
7.	Cattle development	09	12.85
	Total	115	
II.	**Socio-economic and Management Aspects**		
1.	Integrated and holistic development	33	47.14
2.	Improvement in socio-economic status	17	24.28
3.	Human resource development	10	14.28
4.	Generating employment through household component	06	08.57
5.	Cultural and moral development	03	04.28
6.	Need based plan-wise development	03	04.28
7.	Collective community movement	02	02.85
8.	Implementation of plan in time	02	02.85
9.	Development of cluster of villages	01	01.43
	Total	77	

management aspects of the projects. In case of resource conservation, the rainwater harvesting and use was perceived as most important aspect (32.85 %) followed by food crop production (30.00 %), fodder production (21.14%), conservation of soil and water (22.85 %), judicious use of natural resources (20 %), forest (18.47%) and cattle development (12.85%), respectively. In the category of socio-economic and management aspects of watershed development, a great variations in the perception was observed. The project staff showed their maximum concern to integrated and holistic aspect of watershed development (47.14 %) followed by improvement in socio-economic status

(24.28 %) and human resource development (14.28 %). The other factors such as need based plan-wise development, collective community movement and implementation of plan in time which seemed to be very important factors for success of programme, but were perceived as least important by project personnel.

The study reveals that in totality project personnel had more importance to conservation and production components and less to socio-economic and management components of the project. They had varied perception on socio-economic and management aspects but had high value towards integrated and holistic aspect of development.

Perception about Involvement and Nature of Job

The involvement of project personnel in different activities vis-a-vis their nature of job was studied. They were asked on relative importance of their involvement in different activities of watershed project. The informations were presented in Table 4.16.

It was observed that project personnel were not very much clear to their nature of job indicating an absence of clarity in their specific tasks. They listed 21 activities as their nature of job in the project. The personnel were found to be engaged in socio-economic and management aspects and in resource conservation and production measures. The multiple responses were higher in first category followed by second category. The soil and water conservation work, technical service and vegetative development were perceived as somewhat important work. However, all the other activities received less importance to them. In case of their involvement in training, people's movement, and motivation of farmers were received higher attention.

The study reveals that the project personnel had little involvement in some important activities. The watershed being participatory in nature demands total commitment of the staff to involve them as well as involve the beneficiaries in the completion of targets.

Table 4.16 : Perception about the Involvement in Project Activities and Nature of Job of Project Personnel

N=70

Sl. No.	*Perceived activities for involvement and clarity of job*	*No. of Respondents*	*Percentage*
I.	**Socio-economic and management aspects**		
1.	Involvement in training activities	20	28.57
2.	People's movement	09	12.85
3.	Coordinating the project activities	09	12.85
4.	Motivation among farmers	08	11.43
5.	Regular meeting	04	05.71
6.	Converting in local language based programme	04	05.71
7.	Implementing the plan and supervision of work	03	04.28
8.	Use of AV aids in training	02	02.85
9.	Assistance to staff	01	01.43
10.	Working as leader of team	01	01.43
	Total	61	
II.	**Resource conservation and production measures**		
1.	Soil and water conservation work	13	18.57
2.	Technical services	09	12.85
3.	Vegetative development	07	10.00
4.	Demonstrations on crops	06	08.57
5.	Economic improvement	05	07.14
6.	Ponds development	03	04.28
7.	Area development	03	04.28
8.	Survey and project preparation	02	02.85
9.	Subsidy distribution among farmers	02	02.85
10.	Indigenous technological knowledge collection	01	01.43
11.	Algae production	01	01.43
	Total	52	

Training and its Effectiveness

Training as an instrument to provide knowledge, skill and change in attitude on the subject was not properly utilized. It was noticed that 63 per cent personnel received training of the programme whereas 37 per cent did not receive any training on watershed development (Table 4.17).

Table 4.17 : Training received by Project Personnel for Watershed Development

N=70

Sl. No.	Responses	No. of Respondents	Percentage
1.	Training received for watershed development	44	62.85
2.	Training not received for watershed development	26	37.15
	Total	70	100.00

A large number of staff were not having practical experiences of watershed programme. This was one important reason that the programme did not reflect its impact at field level. This needs to be given due attention in the programme.

The responses of project personnel on how to make training on watershed development more effective was analysed and presented in Table 4.18.

Table 4. 18 : Responses of Project Personnel for Effective Trainings

N=70

Sl. No.	Responses	No. of Respondents	Percentage
1.	Practical trainings based on local experience to solve the farmers problem	54	77.14
2.	Organize trainings at village level	39	55.71
3.	Organize trainings at watershed level	22	31.42
4.	Organize trainings at district level	15	21.42
5.	Continuous and intensive trainings	08	11.42
6.	Use of audio-visual aids (charts, poster, film, pamphlet, loudspeaker)	07	10.00
7.	Oral training not class room	06	08.57
8.	Awareness camp and fair in each month	05	07.14
9.	Training on activity/component-wise	04	05.71
10.	Involvement of scientists in training	03	04.28
11.	Developing faith in the programme	02	02.85
12.	Organize awareness programme on local market days	01	01.43
13.	Emphasis on adult to adult training	01	01.43
	Total	167	

The results indicate that as many as 77.14 per cent reported for practical training based on local experiences.

Such training would help to solve farmers problem. About 55.71 per cent reported that such trainings should be organized at village level, about 31.42 and 21.12 per cent of them wanted training at watershed and district level, respectively. They emphasized that training in watershed development should be intensive and on continuous basis (11.42 %). More use of audio-visual aids, oral training not class room training, awareness campaign, fair in each month, training on component-wise, involvement of scientists in training, emphasis on development of faith, awareness programme on market days and adult to adult training were also reported and emphasized by the project personnel to make training really effective in watershed programme.

The preceding discussions reveal that training should be conducted at village or watershed level instead at State Agriculture University and other places. The present system needs to be changed to make the programme a great success. The responses collected on specific location of training are presented in Table 4.19.

Table 4. 19 : Locations of Training received by Project Personnel

N=70

Sl. No.	*Locations for training*	*No. of Respondents*	*Percentage*
1.	State Agriculture Universities (SAUs) and its centre	34	48.57
2.	Workshop by State department	20	28.57
3.	MANAGE, Hyderabad	04	05.71
4.	Watershed level	08	11.42
5.	Non Government Organizations (NGOs)	04	05.71
	Total	70	100

48.57 per cent Project staff received training at State Agricultural University (SAU) and its centre and 28.57 per cent of them had training at workshop organized by State department. Only 5.71 per cent received training at watershed level.

The observations recorded have revealed that training

received by project personnel had no practical utility. The training imparted to project staff was not practical and actual field oriented and, therefore, it did not help in effective management of different activities of watershed projects.

Issues in People's Participation as Perceived by Project Personnel

Organizational Factors in People's Participation

The organizational factors responsible for people's participation were studied in detail. The responses of project staff collected on this aspect are presented in Table 4.20.

Ten major factors were observed which were influencing the people's participation in project. Lack of proper training of grassroot workers, non-consideration of farmers needs, knowledge and suggestions, poor co-ordination among line departments, ego and lack of commitment as reported by 35.71, 21.42, 18.57 and 18.57 per cent of project personnel respectively were considered as important factors responsible for participation in programme. The other factors found important were untimely payment to labour, lack of transport for awareness generation, wrong personal policies, lack of incentives to good worker, low credibility of project staff among villagers and less concern for practicals. All these factors played significant role in getting participation.

The study concludes that the maximum emphasis should be placed on these reported factors and these should be appropriately attended for the success of the project.

Programme related Factors for People's Participation

The efforts were made to find out factors related to programme guidelines, which were responsible for people's participation. Such factors as perceived by the project staff were presented in Table 4.21.

Table 4.20 : Organizational Factors as perceived by Project Personnel in People's Participation

N=70

Sl. No.	*Organizational factors in people's participation*	*No. of Respondents*	*Percentage*
1.	Lack of training to grassroot level people	25	35.71
2.	Non-consideration of farmer's needs knowledge and suggestions in programme implementation	15	21.42
3.	Poor coordination among line departments for multi-disciplinary work	13	18.57
4.	Professionalism, ego, lack of dedication, and corruption in mind (manipulation tendencies) of staff	13	18.57
5.	Untimely fund to payment of labour and wrong fund flow mechanism	08	11.42
6.	Lack of extension work for awareness generation due to unavailability of vehicle	12	17.14
7.	Demotivated staff due to wrong personal policies of State Governments	07	10.00
8.	Low credibility of implementing agency due to past functioning	06	08.57
9.	Lack of incentives to good workers	04	05.71
10.	More teaching and less concern on demonstrations for model at watershed level	02	02.85
	Total	105*	

* Multiple responses.

The data in Table 4.21 reveals that project staff perceived watershed as a new programme with unique objectives and approach (22.85%). They were not used to such work and they treated this also like previous projects and hence programme became governmental programme. About 20 per cent of them had the opinion that programme would not provide immediate and direct benefits and hence, farmers had less initiative. They also perceived that this programme could not be implemented without the help of contractors.

All the ten factors listed were acted negatively in people's participation. Sometimes the local situation demands less or more money for particular work but project personnel cannot do so, due to rigid guidelines. In fact there should have been an effort to dilute the perception of project staff and train them theoretically about the methodology/approach of the project.

Table 4.21 : Programme related Factors as perceived by Project Personnel for People's Participation

N=70

Sl. No.	*Programme related factors in people's participation*	*No. of Respondents*	*Percentage*
1.	This is new programme, with unique objectives and approach against previous schemes	16	22.85
2.	It will not give immediate and direct benefit	14	20.00
3.	Guidelines of programme are rigid and its implementation depends on direct or indirect involvement of contractors	12	17.14
4.	No facilities for tour to visit model watershed project	08	11.42
5.	Lack of programme teaching, training in local language and dialect	07	10.00
6.	Lack of flexibility in expenditure according to field situation	04	5.71
7.	Unrealistic programme, had more formalities and paper work	03	4.28
8.	No provision for advance payment and loan to poor person	03	4.28
9.	Variations in payments for same work among different agencies	02	2.85
10.	Difficult watershed concept and procedure under field conditions	01	1.43
	Total	70*	

* Multiple responses.

The programme of watershed should be realistic and based on actual field situations. It was also experienced that different agencies at the same area had their own norms of expenditure for similar activity and, hence, it created confusions amongst the people. These things could be avoided by proper coordination or merging the guidelines of different programmes in one at grassroot level.

Socio-economic Factors in People's Participation

Altogether 18 socio-economic factors were observed which were influencing people's participation in watershed project (Table 4.22).

The illiteracy and poverty played significant role and affected the psychology of village people subsequently their participation. Another important factor was lack of

Table 4.22 : Socio–economic Issues perceived by Project Personnel

N=70

Sl. No.	*Socio-economic factors in people's participation*	*No. of Respondents*	*Percentage*
1.	Lack of basic education/illiteracy in people	42	60.00
2.	Lack of knowledge of programme objectives and their benefit to village people	33	47.14
3.	Poor economic condition of village people	32	45.71
4.	Lost faith in Govt. work due to their previous functioning	20	28.57
5.	Demotivated, prejudiced and suppressed people have little courage to interact with staff	12	17.14
6.	Prevailing perception in people of getting cash and quick benefit from government programme	08	11.42
7.	Social chain of marriages, customs, conflicts and alcoholism restrict to think on development	08	11.42
8.	Soil and water erosion perceived as natural and on-going process need not to be improved	02	02.85
9.	Fear of unsocial elements in village people and in staff	02	02.85
10.	Development is not free from politics in village	02	02.85
11.	Fear in farmers that land will go in Govt. possession	02	02.85
12.	Less equity concern and more fraction in society	01	01.43
13.	Lack of interest in contribution of money	01	01.43
14.	Migration of people for wages	01	01.43
15.	Majority had no faith in *mitra kisan*	01	01.43
16.	Poor marketing facilities for sale of new commodities	01	01.43
17.	Indebtedness of Govt. loan keep away from other programme	01	01.43
18.	Lack of visit by progressive farmers to model watershed	01	01.43
	Total	170*	

* Multiple responses.

awareness of objectives and benefit of the programme among the people. About 28.57 per cent of the project staff reported that village people had lost their faith in government system. About 17.14 per cent of them felt that farmers had remained demotivated, prejudiced and suppressed had no courage. This situation might be due to accumulated affect of first two socio-economic factors i.e. illiteracy and poverty did not provide courage to interact with the staff in the meetings. The other factors were wrong perception of people of getting cash or kind benefit from government schemes and social chain of marriages, customs, conflicts and alcoholism.

It was also noted that soil and water erosion was perceived by the farmers as a natural and on-going process do not require any interfere, social situation such as terrorism, equity concern in social status had divided the society, fear that the land will go in government's possession, lack of interest in contribution of money for community work, frequent migration for wages, lack of faith in *mitra kisans* due to their negative attitude. Indebtedness of government loan kept away from the project, lack of provisions for visits to model watershed projects etc. were responsible for poor implementation of project.

All these factors appear to be is strong enough to force the people away from the programme. A concerted effort is required to deal with these issues and mitigate them. Frequent open discussion and involvement of key people and Panchayat members may help to arouse interest among farmers to take initiative for their benefits under the project. The role of project staff is very crucial in this matter.

Issues of Watershed Management as perceived by the Scientists

The agriculture scientists and experts concerned with watershed management research and development were contacted for the purpose. Interaction with 45 such personnel from ICAR and SAUs was held with a questionnaire. These people were from the categories of Scientist, Senior scientist, Principal scientist, retired Directors and ADGs levels. Responses were collected on organizational programme related and socio-economic aspect of watershed development and presented in Tables 4.23, 4.24, and 4.25.

Organizational Issues

The information on organizational aspect of watershed was analyzed and presented in Table 4.23. The data reveal that majority of scientists 46.66 per cent showed their concern on wrong execution of project without associating people in planning and development process. About 37.77 per cent of them observed lack of co-ordination amongst multi-sectarian departments for watershed project due to policy, professionalism and ego problem of the staff, about 13.33 per cent of the scientists perceived that there are lack of trained, motivated and good staff for watershed development programme. The same old staff of soil and water conservation was directed to carry out this work and, hence, the programme fails. The other organizational factors were observed to be unsystematic, imperfect, causal implementation (8.88%), lack of co-ordination with research (6.66 %), project approach is not very much integrated (4.44 %), need for creation of awareness about project (4.44 %), and ineffectiveness of implementation agency (2.22%).

Watershed being innovative programme of participatory nature demands special attention on these issues. For the success of the programme, these need proper attention. The staff involved should be provided adequate training and dedicated workers, and they should be properly rewarded. Programme should also provide freedom for project staff to take initiative and decision on proper course of involving people in the programme.

Table 4.23 : Organizational Issues perceived by Scientists

N=45

Sl. No.	*Organizational issues*	*No. of Scientists*	*Percentage*
1.	Project personnel fault in execution without, associating people in planning and development process	21	46.66
2.	Lack of co-ordination in line-departments due to policy, professionalism and ego problem	17	37.77
3.	Lack of trained, motivated and good staff	06	13.33
4.	Need to create more awareness	06	13.33
5.	Implementation is unsystematic and casual	04	08.88
6.	Lack of co-ordination with scientists	03	06.66
7.	Project approach is not integrated	02	04.44
8.	Ineffective implementing agency	02	04.44
	Total	61*	

* Multiple responses.

Programme related Issues

The programme related issues were tried to know from scientists and their responses recorded are presented in Table 4.24.

Table 4.24 : Programme related Issues perceived by Scientists

N=45

Sl, No.	*Programme related issues*	*No. of Scientists*	*Percentage*
1.	Watershed programme is target oriented and content guided from top level	09	20.00
2.	Require a need based village level people's approach	08	17.77
3.	Sectorial funding for achieving physical targets	05	11.11
4.	No priority in people's participation in the programme	04	08.88
5.	Less emphasis on trees and fodder	03	06.66
6.	Indigenous knowledge based development programme	03	06.66
7.	Lack of appropriate technologies	02	04.44
8.	More emphasis in programme on collection of scientific information	02	04.44
9.	Special incentives must be given to those research scientists who are involved in development work	02	04.44
10.	Good efforts through programme in terms of adoption	01	02.22
11.	Watershed programme is scientifically sound	01	02.22
12.	Regional research scientists should be involved in implementation process	01	02.22
	Total	41*	

* Multiple responses.

It appears from the Table 4.24 that as many as 20.00 per cent of the scientists felt that the watershed programme was target oriented and its contents were often guided from the top. About 17.77 per cent of them realized that the programme required a need based village level people's approach. This would ensure people's involvement in implementation process. They suggested that there should not be sectorial funding for achieving physical targets. About 8.88 per cent of them found that in the programme, the people's participation had no priority, which was the basic requirement of watershed development. Other issues of programme were related to emphasis on collection of scientific information and lack of emphasis on tree and fodder crops and lack of appropriate technologies. The scientists also observed that watershed programme should make best use of indigenous knowledge and practices. There should be involvement of scientists and regional research stations directly in the programme and the work of scientists duly rewarded. They felt that watershed programme is scientifically sound and there should be concerted efforts on the part of the project staff to involve the farmers and promote scientific technologies for the benefit of the people.

All the 12 issues perceived by the scientists are very relevant. This can only be ensured if the project staff are properly trained, given freedom for work and closely monitored by the senior staff. There should not be any fixed targets for any activities. Let each should take its own time in perfection and completion through participatory approach. Motivation of staff is essential in this endeavour.

Socio-economic Issues

The socio-economic issues affecting the implementation of watershed project were analyzed from the scientist's point of view and result is presented in Table 4.25. It is apparent that "people are illiterate and need proper training" was the major issue as perceived by 15.55 per cent of scientists. The other important issues were related to resource poor condition and want of immediate, economic benefits, proper efforts and time in persuading farmers and urban effect in rural areas. They observed that these socio-economic issues were very important and maximum efforts should be put to these issues for the success of watershed development project.

Training can be one instrument to educate about the programme. Due to poverty reason, farmers' demand was for quick benefit. Persuasion process to farmers will take time and it is also difficult.

Table 4.25 : Socio-economic Issues perceived by Scientists

N=45

Sl. No.	Socio-economic issues	No. of Scientists	Percentage
1.	People are uneducated they need proper training	07	15.55
2.	They are poor, have no inputs and need quick economic benefit	06	13.33
3.	Difficult to persuade farmers it will take time	04	08.88
4.	Urban effect in rural areas	02	04.44
	Total	19	

* Multiple responses.

Performance of Non Government Organization (NGO) in Watershed Programme–A Case

Background of a NGO

Mr. Sharad Joshi established a NGO, Centre for Community Economics and Development Consultants Society (CECOE DECON) in 1985. Joshi had master degree in social work. The NGO is also known as *Agro-action* among the farmers and located at village Shelki Dungri of Chaksu Sub-division 34 km from Jaipur in Rajasthan. The operational area was Chaksu and Phagi Tehsil of Jaipur district comprising of 433 villages with a population of 2.19 lakh. More than 20 schemes of rural development were running very successfully through the NGO in these areas. The motto of NGO was "where action speaks louder than words". That means they don't believe in propaganda and paper work, rather in actual action.

Organizational Structure for Soil Water Conservation Programme

The organization had developed a three-tier system to implement the soil and water conservation activities. The Director of NGO was head of the soil conservation unit and he was supported by secretary of organization. Besides there was one programme coordinator and another chief coordinator. Programme coordinator was immediate boss of community motivators as men as well as women. Agril. engineering wing, soil-testing laboratory, training cell and audio-visual unit of NGO were assisting the soil and water conservation programme as when and where required. There was good coordination in this multi-disciplinary team.

Staff and their Facilities

The organization had more than 100 of staff working at different ladders i.e. from headquarters to village level. The staff members at headquarters had good offices for work. To maintain the accounts of NGO, he had appointed retired persons from government. These people had keen desire to serve the local people.

The newly recruited person first get posted in village and after 4-5 years asked to join at headquarters. If their performances are not up to the mark, they would not get promotion and time span for fieldwork would increase. Some of the project personnel with urban background do face problems in staying and working in villages. In such a situation, most of them either leave the job after few months or change their life style according to local situation. As it was observed that the character of person posted in village and his dedication to work are given due priority.

The NGO prefer local people because these people had good rapport and deep insight to local situation.

However availability of such good workers was difficult sometimes. Another problem the NGO faced was that fresh or little experienced person usually join the organization and after gaining good experience in 4-5 years they left the organization. Some of these people either initiated their own organization or got selected for other jobs. Thus, incompetent staff stays for longer period and in this way, programme got setback. The NGO staff had poor opportunity for training and linkage with research organization. No library facilities and other means of informations were available to them. The NGO authorities were not aware to source of availability of technology. Staff members also felt English language as barrier for their development. Because of good working climate, the staff had service motives. They had personnel touch to farmers. Such motives were usually lacking in government. For "people's participation the staff are required to come down to the level of village people" and serve them rather control them as was found in government system. This line of action to people's mobilization worked in NGO.

Community motivators had been provided vehicles viz. moped and bicycle, so they could comfortably visit 5 villages allotted to them. These motivators used to stay in project area. In the village, women community motivators were more successful in persuading small groups of women farmers. It was also observed that women farmers had equal chance of participation in the meetings conducted in villages and headquarters of NGO. The training courses especially designed for women were frequently organized at NGO headquarters. In these courses women community motivator played the facilitator's role that helped in creating good learning environment. Due to low level of education more visual aids were used to educate the women farmers. They were showed video films on bio-diversity, watershed management etc. The NGO had good collection of posters. These posters either purchased or donated by national and international agencies.

The accommodation had been provided to staff at NGO headquarters that helped to the organization in many ways. They also had good dormitory for trainees and food service through mess. Games and recreation facilities at headquarters were provided for benefit of staff. Organizing evening prayer composed for cause of rural development was a regular feature of organization.

Weekly schedule of activities circulated among the members showing their targets. The monitoring and evaluation of their work did in a systematic manner. Organization used those techniques to solve the farmer's problem as they were observing in day-to-day life through formal and informal discussion amongst staff member as well as farmers. Such experiences used to directly link with formulation of new projects. When these projects were submitted for foreign donor, they get immediate sanction with little bit improvement in expression of language.

Organizational Climate and Collective Decision

The observations were collected at a programme on celebration of new year's day organized at headquarters of NGO. The staff posted in the villages under different schemes were the participants. On this occasion, all the schemes of NGO were evaluated in the presence of the entire members in the meeting, criticism and suggestions were openly made in a friendly environment. Every one got aware of work to others. The assigned work was presented showing each activity and new targets were set. Promotion policy and increase in salaries were also announced. Special packages were given to hard and sincere workers. One interesting case of a staff member Shri Shardananda was discussed.

Shardananda a young man of 35 years, having diploma in social work, joined the NGO for welfare of the society. He worked for eight years with Udaipur based NGO Seva Mandir. Later on, he joined the CE COE DECON. He was getting Rs. 3000 per month as salary. He was always short of money due to drinking habit and used to ask for money from his colleagues. This habit made him unpopular among the NGO staff and his family was unhappy. Staff and management of NGO imposed certain sanctions like delay in his promotion. This sanction played vital role. It was observed that slowly Shardananda was getting rid of drinking habit. Such sanctions and persuasive attitude are rarely seen in public sector organizations.

Linkage with Research Stations, Development Departments and Abroad

The NGO has developed linkages with research stations and was conducting demonstrations on crops under expert's supervision. They were paid as honorarium for the same. In a meeting organized at Jai Singh Pura, the Block Development Officer (BDO) while discussing, narrated all the development programmes and their benefits to the farmers. The result of the meeting was encouraging. Next day few farmers visited the block office to get the application forms for sanction of loan. In an earlier attempt, the NGO arranged loan application forms and asked to farmers to fill it. But nobody came forward to fill the forms and avail facilities of loan as they were not fully convinced. The meeting of NGO with experts, BDO and the farmers worked, as potential tool to motivate the farmers and result as stated was obvious.

The NGO had maintained linkages with foreign schools through some organization. The youth and adults from Canada and other countries used to visit and learn the rural scenario in supervision of selected NGOs like it. These delegates stayed for few months at the NGO's guest room. Facilities of computer, vehicle, food etc. are provided to these delegates. The staff of NGO also feels proud to work and stay with these foreign delegates. The employees of CE COE DECON also visited Nepal by plane that created high motivation and commitment in lower level staff. The reasons for the success and failure summarized as under :

(i) Small organizational structure,
(ii) Strict supervision and frequent evaluation of work,
(iii) Better coordination in team work,

(iv) Flexibility in policy and linkages with development departments,
(v) Weekly schedule of meetings with farmers,
(vi) Consideration of local experiences in developing plan,
(vii) Initial posting of staff at village level,
(viii) Good training infrastructure and use of audio-visual in training,
(ix) Service motive in staff members,
(x) Recruitment of experienced retired persons,
(xi) Staff sets their own targets to achieve goals,
(xii) Promotion and incentive based on sincerity to work,
(xiii) Staff was not technically competent,
(xiv) More dropout from organization,
(xv) Less opportunity for training to staff, and
(xvi) Good linkage to abroad and opportunities to foreign visit.

Soil and Water Conservation Work and Tree Plantation

Soil and water conservation was the major activity of the organization. NGO had already completed one project by World Bank assistance on integrated watershed management, DRDA also selected CE COE DECON as implementing agency for watershed project under their new guidelines. A Sweden based agency (SWISS) had given funds for watershed development work. Presently, they were working in 15 villages for soil and water conservation programme. It was noticed that work had been done under different activities in sectarian form i.e. forestry extension programme, land reclamation programme, concrete gravity dam, farm field bunding in 3,000 ha in 80 villages. The farm bunding did generate 40-50 mandays of employment per hectare. So far six (6) concrete gravity dam were constructed between 1985 to 1991 benefiting 41 villages, 250 farmers and 400 ha of land. Through the forestry programme, people of 12 villages were directly benefited and 15,000 mandays of work were created. Black fertile soil of ponds was mixed with sandy soil was another activity. About 100 ha land of small and marginal farmers was reclaimed by this technique.

Project staff had chosen site for plant nursery adjoining to panchayat building and school. The school children were given responsibilities to irrigate the nursery from time to time. In this way, school children also developed positive feeling to environment. The NGO personnel fenced the pasture land for afforestation and planted forestry saplings. The plants could not survive due to irrigation problem. Further, the quality of irrigation water was poor. They decided to make arrangements of water for irrigation through tanker from a distant of 2-3 km, the tanker was to be arranged by the NGO while tractor by village people. However, the farmer did not agree. For termite problem in plants, the NGO arranged insecticide but could not be used due to unavailability of water for making solution. Farmers were not happy with NGO personnel, as they could not protect the forestry plants. The survival percentage of plant was 10-20 per cent only. As a whole, the important factors were :

(i) Sectorian work,
(ii) Field bunding,
(iii) Use of local available labours,
(iv) Mechanism for people's participation such as, involvement of village schools, social fencing, water for irrigation and sharing money with people, and
(v) Good efforts but less success.

Socio-Economic Factors

The NGO was promoting informal groups as Village Development Society (VDS) and Mahila Mandals (MMs). These groups were helping to NGO staff in organizing labour, sharing inputs, and settling disputes through negotiation.

The training and *chaupal* were used for generating awareness through help of community motivator. They were selecting people and setting conditions for participation after explaining the programme.

Staff members used to attend *chaupal,* wherein seasonal problems were discussed regularly. Some common music instruments and meal were arranged by NGO personnel that used to help in gathering people. These meetings were arranged weekly or fortnightly on their turn in all selected villages.

A stereotype system was observed in *chaupal* with assumptions that the people would come, take seat, listen and go. The available proceedings of one-year meetings were analyzed from the register maintained by the NGO staff. It was observed that the purpose of meetings was agriculture development by the use of sustainable practices. The analysis showed that on an average, 12-15 members participated in meeting from beginning to last. The problems discussed were also the same from beginning to last. The general problems were emphasized more on non-functioning of community handpump and no help from government to rectify the same. This problem remained as such till last because of lack of initiative to take action. There was less discussion about objectives of project for which these meetings were organized.

Participatory Training — An Observation

Sharda Nanda was incharge of training cell at NGO. He developed his own line of action as a trainer inside classroom or conducting training in villages. NGO personnel organized one training at village Jai Singh Pura. The objective of training was "to develop leadership quality among the farmers" so that the village people could take over the work of watershed after withdrawal of the project.

Observations were made by attending two days of

training held at village Jai Singh Pura. The venue of training was the primary school building of village. About 20 participants in equal ratio of men and women were present in meeting. The trainer Sharda played a communication game of PRA technique to convey his message by use of white chart paper, sketch pen, cello tape with support of school wall.

Before starting the training session, a prayer of NGO was performed. The prayer was composed in local tune and having deep sense of devotion towards village development. Later in meeting Sharda Nanda narrated different points of prayer relating with goal of training session. A few points such as "everybody wants development, it is difficult to churn ghee from the milk to prepare ghee, one needs to keep milk first for heating etc. Similarly two days of training would make participants to apply their mind to think on development. This was true that participants were doing the development work, no doubt but the speed may be 60, 40 but not 100, it can take 8-10 years to reach the desired goal. So here the need is to "accelerate the process of development." Such types of statements get attention of participants very quickly.

The exercise played by Sharda through a sketch of a "sad man" drawn on chart paper hanging on wall. The sketch of sad man was gunned by number of arrows. These arrows were told to participants as people's enemies were acting as barriers in development. These barriers might also be own luck of farmers or government people working for development or neighbourers personal interests or people etc. Who were the enemies and why the man felt sad, could group member tell? — asked by trainer. Now the participants were observing the situation, what the trainer really wanted to convey in their message. In the meeting, the farmers put forth a number of problems one by one such as problem of pasture, water, boundary, non-functioning of handpump, link road to village, hospital for cattle, forest department creating problems etc. These were common problems told by male participants. After breaking the group between male and female, few other problems emerged from women such as problem related to no dam, need of sweet water for drinking, need to connect each house with water tank, need a hospital for children, pucca road, etc.

What would be the benefit if problems were solved one by one and the sad man would become happier. If road comes to village, farmers can get better price of bajra, can grow vegetables, bus can come to village, easy movement of tractors from village to field. Such benefits could easily be achieved for a single problem by removing one arrow.

Who would approach for road work? May be the PWD, achieved for a Road department or Agricultural Marketing department and they will do their jobs. That is their duty, they would come to village and do all required things for road making. Now trainer Sharda Nanda took his seat, OK, these three departments would see the road work. A silence was seen among the group members and then murmuring began among the group members and the conclusion drawn as "No unity in the village, everybody talking but nobody taking initiative to work."

Sharda Nanda spoke again that it was sure that whole village would not come for taking the initiative or action, at least 20 per cent should come forward. The development department of the Jaipur would never dream for these problems. If "cock will speak, there would be dawn". If "child will cry milk will be served to him." The government staff are getting their salary and doing their routine duty. They do not bother only to one village. Think peacefully "what" should be the way to solve present problem. "In *Satyuga,* it was decided in *Mahabharat* that the battle would be closed at 5 P.M., it used to close according to decision. Now is *Kalyuga,* those having stick in hand or coming forward can do better." Government policies are different, government is ready to help those people who want to help themselves. The duty of village people is to come forward, reach that level and take advantage of different schemes.

At the end, three people were selected as representatives to approach the development department. The village people decided to share the fair of these people and cooperate in other matters. In this way the meeting came to an end.

The above observations suggest a need of good facilitators to mobilize the people. A highly educated person cannot be successful at grassroot level. Training module for each situation would be different and such module can be developed through better coordination between professional trainer and local motivator. The following issues emerged from the above observation as lessons to be used for sustainable development of the people and village :

(i) Village level workshops/trainings,
(ii) Participation of women,
(iii) Use of cost effective material in training,
(iv) Practical experience of staff and the people,
(v) Local songs, phrases and idioms in farmers' meetings,
(vi) Trainer capability to attract the farmers attention for conveying the message,
(vii) Encouraging people's participation in setting disputes and developing actions plans, and
(viii) Role play exercise.

The reasons for success of a Non Government Organization (NGO) in watershed were many. The important is small organizational structure, strict supervision, good facilities for staff especially to visit the farmers but less salary, division of labour, better coordination in team, flexibility in policy and linkages with development department.

Technologically, NGO was not sound but had better approach for technology dissemination. At village level informal groups and regular night meetings of farmers with music, good training facilities and better use of AV aids, convincing the farmers through special exercises were the specific reasons to recognize.

Comparison of Issues

Comparison of Government Organization (GO) and Non-Government Organization (NGO)

The implementation of watershed projects run by Government and Non Government Organization in the same locality were analyzed and compared. The organizational, technological and socio-economic aspects were observed in both the agencies to see what was their approach in development of watershed project. The results are presented in Table 4.26.

It appears from Table 4.26 that there was a distinct variation in the functioning of Government and NGO in watershed project. Comparatively the NGO was found to have serious concern for the proper implementation of watershed project. The programme and activities were quite flexible to meet the need and expectations of people in NGO functioning, whereas it was less flexible in government functioning. Overall, the issues related to organizational, technological and socio-economic aspects of watershed were adequately managed in NGO whereas in government it was found very causal. The very purpose of involving the people was lost in government functioning.

Comparative Degree of Importance on Perceived Issues by Farmers, Project Personnel and Scientists

An attempt was made to compare the perceived issues of the farmers, project personnel and scientists as experienced in project implementation. The perceived issues were categorized in Organizational, Technological and Socio-economic aspects of watershed project implementation were presented in Tables 4.27, 4.28, 4.29 respectively. The issues were rated as high (H), medium (M)) and low (L) in

Table 4.26 : Comparison of Issues with Government and Non Government Organization

Sl. No.	*Major issues*	*GO*	*NGO*
I.	**Organizational Issues**		
1.	Organizational structure	Big and less effective	Small and effective
2.	Supervision of work	Ad hoc	Close and frequent
3.	Facilities for staff	Poor	Very good
4.	Salary of staff	Good	Not so good
5.	Coordination in team	Very poor	Very good
6.	Flexibility in policy	Less	High
7.	Linkage with development departments	More but unused	Less but used
8.	Meetings with farmers	Rare and not scheduled	Very frequent and fixed
9.	Service motives in staff members	Less and present in few	Very high
10.	Training infrastructure	Good but not appropriately used	Good and adequately used
11.	Training of staff on participatory method	No	Yes
12.	Technical competency of staff	Average	Good
13.	Incentive to good work	No	Yes
14.	Promotional policy	Rigid and demotivational	Flexible and rewarding
15.	Programme implementation	Stereotype and target oriented	Participatory oriented and people's way
16.	Consideration of local experiences and practices in developing plan	Less concern	More concern
17.	Frequent and open evaluation of work	Rare but open	Very frequent and open
18.	Linkage with local research stations	Good but not properly used	Poor but properly used
II.	**Technological Issues**		
1.	Sectorial work	Less concern	More concern
2.	Field bunding	Priority	Less priority
3.	Use of local available labours	Less	Good involvement
4.	Programmes for people's participation	Very poor	Very good
5.	Involvement of village schools	No	Good involvement
6.	Sharing benefits with people	Poor management management	Adequate
7.	Programme of immediate benefit	Yes, poorly organized	Yes, appropriately organized
8.	Awareness creation	Very poor	Very good

(Contd.)

Table 4.26 : (Contd.)

Sl. No.	*Major issues*	*GO*	*NGO*
III.	**Socio-economic Issues**		
1.	Development of informal groups	Poor effort	Good effort with emphasis
2.	Gender concern	Low	Very high
3.	Daily work report	No	Yes
4.	Settling special disputes	No effort	Good effort
5.	Condition for participation	Poor	Very high
6.	*Choupal* with farmers	Unused	Used
7.	Village level workshops/ training	Occasional	Fortnightly and fixed
8.	Concern of staff for involving people	Little concern	High concern
9.	Selection of *mitra kisans*	Personal & autocratic	Democratic
10.	Practical experience of staff	Poor	Very good
11.	Use of local songs, phrases and idioms in farmers meetings	No	Always

category according to the degree of importance for the personnel.

The analysis of Table 4.27 shows that more than 60 per cent organizational issues had high (H) degree of importance to all three categories of personnel means farmers, project personnel and scientists. It means these were very important issues at each level of project. In general, responses of project personnel were in medium category according to degree of importance, which means they followed middle path to work. The concern of scientists for first six issues was high (H).

As shown in Table 4.28 that programme/guidelines related issues had more importance to project personnel as most of the issues rated in medium to high categories by them. Scientists may not have the knowledge of project or they think that programme is all right. So most of the factors rated low to medium importance by scientists.

The last Table 4.29 shows that project personnel and farmers respectively had medium to high importance for socio-economic factors as compared to scientists as they had medium to low importance.

Table 4. 27 : Comparison of Perceived Organizational Issues

Sl. No.	*Perceived organizational issues*	*Degree of importance*		
		Farmers	*Project personnel*	*Scientists*
1.	Farmers' needs, knowledge and suggestions were not considered in implementation	H	M	H
2.	Lack of awareness about the programme	H	M	H
3.	Casual planning and implementation	H	M	H
4.	Poor coordination among extension agencies	L	H	H
5.	Lack of dedication among project staff	H	M	H
6.	Untrained staff	L	M	H
7.	Frequent transfer of project staff	H	M	M
8.	Social aggressiveness of local leaders causes insecurity among project staff	L	H	L
9.	Total dependency on field staff for implementation	H	M	L
10.	Low credibility of implementing agency	H	M	H
11.	Complex procedure and policy of funding	H	H	L
12.	Faulty procedure in selection of *mitra kisans*	H	H	M
13.	Benefits mostly availed by rich farmers	H	H	L
14.	Contract system of work at field	M	H	H
15.	Lack of basic data for planning	M	H	M
16.	Deteriorating organizational climate	M	M	H

H–High, M–Medium, L–Low

Table 4.28 : Comparison of Perceived Programme related Issues

Sl. No.	*Perceived organizational issues*	*Degree of importance*		
		Farmers	*Project personnel*	*Scientists*
1.	Watershed is new programme	L	H	L
2.	Target oriented programme	H	M	H
3.	Sectorial funding in programme	H	H	H
4.	No priority on people's participation	M	H	H
5.	Unrealistic objective and more paper work	L	H	M

(Contd.)

Table 4.28 : (Contd.)

6.	Rigid programme guidelines	L	H	M
7.	No provision for loan in programme	H	H	H
8.	Unavailability of inputs at watershed level	M	H	L
9.	Lack of provision for funds for visits	M	H	M
10.	Emphasis should be on trees and fodder	M	M	H
11.	To be indigenous knowledge based programme	M	L	H
12.	Lack of appropriate technology	M	M	H

H–High, M–Medium, L–Low

Table 4. 29 : Comparison of Perceived Socio-economic Issues

Sl. No.	*Perceived organizational issues*	*Degree of importance*		
		Farmers	*Project personnel*	*Scientists*
1.	Illiteracy and poverty	L	H	H
2.	Unawareness of objectives and benefit of programme	H	H	H
3.	Lost faith in government functioning	H	M	L
4.	Demotivated, prejudiced and suppressed people	M	H	H
5.	Farmers were bound with customs, conflicts and alcoholism	M	H	L
6.	Continuous migration of farmers for wages	H	H	M
7.	Low status of women	L	M	H
8.	Terrorism in society	M	H	L
9.	Grassroot level politics in development	H	H	L
10.	Lack of conflicts resolution system	H	H	M
11.	Problem to share benefits	L	H	H
12.	Lack of interest for development on Common Property Resources (CPR)	M	H	M
13.	Soil and water erosion perceived as natural and ongoing process	M	M	L
14.	Due to repayment loan farmers keep himself away from project	M	M	H
15.	Prevailing perception in people of getting cash and quick benefit from government programme	H	H	L
16.	Negative attitude in adoption of technology	M	H	M
17.	Failure of technology loses farmers faith	H	H	M
18.	Partial adoption of technologies	M	M	M

H–High, M–Medium, L–Low

5 Summary and Conclusions

Watershed development is considered an important project in natural resource conservation and upliftment of socio-economic conditions of the people. The Government of India launched a nationwide programme i.e., National Watershed Development Project for Rainfed Area (NWDPRA) during 1991. About 196 projects were sanctioned in Rajasthan State under this programme. The project, which was launched with innovative approach of people's participation, did not meet the desired goals. In order to know the extension and management issues influencing the effective implementation of NWDPRA, the proposed study was launched with the following objectives :

Objectives

1. To examine goals, programme, structure and functioning of watershed projects.
2. To study organizational, technological and socio-economic issues in implementation of watershed project.
3. To study the perception/experiences of project personnel and farmers on selected aspects of watershed development.
4. To compare the issues and suggest appropriate strategy for implementation of project.

To achieve the objectives data were collected from

Central, State, district, watershed and finally from village level. The selected watershed i.e., Bara Padampura was located 35 km from Jaipur on Jaipur-Tonk road near to Chaksu. The total area of watershed project was 6310.70 ha and Rs. 2.34 crore was sanctioned for development under the Eighth Plan. The sample for study was 190 that consists policy makers, researchers, project personnel, key farmers (*mitra kisans*) beneficiaries and non-beneficiaries, personnel from Non Government Organization. The case study method and exploratory survey were used as data collection devices. The technique of rapport building, participant and non-participant observation, informal and formal discussion, group discussion were also used. The collected quantitative and qualitative data were analysed for appropriate interpretations. The major findings of the study are summarized as under :

A. Programme Awareness in Farmers

1. The contractors were selected as *mitra kisans*. They were the main source of awareness as reported by 53.33 per cent of farmers. Panchayat members and progressive farmers had only 23.33 and 10.00 per cent of shares as source of awareness. Mass media and other personnel of government had poor role in awareness generation among farmers about watershed programme.
2. The awareness among farming community about the project was maximum for soil conservation followed by pasture development, crop production and animal husbandry component, respectively. Among the conservation measures, the maximum, awareness of farmers (60%) was for bunding measures. Vegetative measures like *munja* transplantation (40%), *ipomea* transplantation (33.33%) and new ponds (26.66 %) were other measures of awareness for the farmers.

Few people knew gully plug, checkdams and repairing of old ponds.

3. The awareness of plantation on pasture land was observed by 40 per cent of farmers of the area, digging of pits and contour vegetative hedge (33.33%) each. The awareness was very low for making 'V' ditch (20%) and plantation of Ber (*Zizyphus mauritiana*) and Subabul (*Leucaena leucocephola*) (10%).
4. As many as 40 per cent of farmers were aware of improved seed distribution programme followed by 26.66 per cent of diammonium phosphate. About 20 per cent had awareness of distribution of urea and compost pit making. Hardly, 16.66 per cent of them were aware of distribution of sprayers and dusters.
5. With regard to animal husbandry programme, the maximum 53.33 per cent awareness was for cattle fair, followed by chaffcutter distribution (26.66%), *gopals* working in project (13.33%), artificial insemination and castration programme (10%).

The overall awareness of different programmes was observed to be very low. Awareness of the programme is very first stage of people's participation. The maximum awareness was for soil conservation activities whereas the minimum was for cattle development work. Farmers were thinking that government people were doing some work in and around the villages, means farmers were aware to only few activities of the project in very disintegrated way. They had very deteriorated picture of the watershed approach as a policy maker commented that "at initiation stage the watershed concept had hundred per cent value and at execution only 15 per cent". The programme did not involve people and was running on contract basis. Even though the farmers were aware about the part and parcel of the programme. Consequently, the very purpose of involving people was defeated.

B. Issues in Watershed Project Implementation

The study analyzed the organizational, technological and socio-economic issues in implementation of watershed project.

(I) *Organizational Issues at Field Level*

1. The project implementation was in *ad hoc* manner and in hurry without constituting the committees. The panchayat and others views were not considered. The known persons were chosen to personal benefits and such persons helped in sharing all sorts of views under the project. Only result oriented major activities of project were started at beginning through contractors and supervisor did not disclose the programme in public knowingly.
2. The *mitra kisans* were not properly selected. The *mitra kisans* were working for self motives and there was no concern for observing the procedure and involving village people in the programme.
3. The wrong perception for *mitra kisans* was due to their personal motives. They did not like the advantages of the project to be shared by the people. The decision making was centred in few hands.
4. Labourers of the project area did not have feelings that this was their programme. They had only concerns for their wages through work.
5. The awareness generation was not effective. Instead of creating proper awareness about project, unrealistic expectations were created in farmers meetings by the project staff. These acted adversely and the people lost faith in the programme when their expectations were not fulfilled.
6. The rich people had good linkage to urban areas vis-a-vis government offices and were front runner in

programme implementation. Initially project staff had fear in mind from these people and subsequently, decided to implement the activities through these people.

The study revealed that at the time of selection of *mitra kisans*, democratic process was ignored and personal relations dominated. The rich farmers developed good rapport with project personnel and succeeded to take some work in watershed project as contractors and not as beneficiaries. There was no proper training of the *mitra kisans* and work facilities were poor. The perception of *mitra kisans* differed on people's participation as they think that "involving people was inviting trouble". The rich farmers largely took benefits of the programme.

The animal husbandry component was not successful due to improper training of *mitra kisans* and lack of facilities at field level. Duplication of efforts was also observed in different activities at village level, which created confusion among villagers about the jurisdiction of different agencies. It was also observed that involvement of city/town based migrated people could be an asset for their own village development in mobilizing people. These people may be more helpful in the selection of actual *mitra kisans* and have support of local people. From the above facts it is apparent that in implementation of watershed projects, the prescribed guidelines were ignored. The participatory process was lacking and the consideration was to fulfil the project target by any means. Local poor people were not oriented about programme as they used to go for work in other places to get higher wages.

The people should be allowed to select their representatives as *mitra kisans*. At village level, an appropriate plan needs to be prepared by the village people. The development agencies are to act as facilitator to achieve this end. This way the activities of different agencies may be spell out and coordinated to ensure positive mobilization and also to avoid duplication of efforts.

(II) Organizational Issues with Implementing Agency

1. Proper survey was not carried out at the beginning of the project and the information collected from secondary sources were not updated since long and were unrealistic.
2. Faith of local people in the project staff had its own value. Once a staff creates a climate for change at grassroot level, he should not be changed, rather should be rewarded for his good work. This would help in building confidence in both project staff and the people but the results observed were otherwise. There was frequent transfer of project staff on personnel or political basis that is not desirable. The transfer policy of the Government affected the faith and attitude of other project staff negatively.
3. Good behaviour, friendly approach, honesty, sincerity for work, team spirit, knowledge of work, hard working, more time for encouraging harmony in village people, frequent meeting with farmers were observed important characteristics required to win the faith and mobilize the village people by project staff. These characteristics affected the implementation in their own way.
4. Frustration in staff was also due to poor support from concerned departments and lack of transport facilities. The tendency among project personnel of whom or which agency would get credit of work was dominated. As a result, the project received poor coordination of multidisciplinary agencies for the work.
5. The senior staff was more dependent on field level staff, who were technically less competent, but took all important decisions at field level.
6. The watershed development projects had causal way of planning, planning without considering actual facts, planning by inexperienced hands etc. In

practice, money decided the plan, not the plan decided the money to solve the problems.

7. Trial and error method in fund flow was observed from government side and the procedure finally adopted was more complex and caused delay in wage payment.

The situation indicates that there was bureaucracy in the system and non-congenial climate in the organization that influenced the spirit for watershed development. Interpretation shows that certain policy issues affected the implementation drastically. The planning was not according to farmer's need and it depended on availability of funds in programmes. At the beginning of the project, proper survey was not carried out and the information collected from secondary sources was not updated since long. Due to poor supervision, field staff chalked out the plan on their own that proved to be wrong and lot of money was wasted in this way. More dependence on field level staff was observed that caused loss of the initiative for work.

(III) Technological Issues in Implementation

1. The important technologies of the project were observed as bunds and ponds making, repair of old ponds, gully plugs and check dam construction, transplantation of *munja* and *ipomea* as vegetative barriers, plantation on pasture land, fruit tree plantation, high yielding varieties (HYV) demonstration, use of fertilizer, chaffcutter machines, income generation activities, artificial insemination and castration in cattle.
2. No serious attempts were made for the adoption of appropriate technology. The advocated technologies were partially adopted and their total benefits were not realized. This in turn created problem in the spread of technology. The technological failure acted

negatively and farmers lost faith in the technologies and project staff.

3. Most of the work was done by tractors and where tractor was not possible to reach in field, labour was used for watershed activities. The intention of field level project staff and contractor was to earn more money.
4. Due to lack of proper facilities for veterinary work, the cattle development component did not make good impact. Local government officials of animal husbandry department were found to have indifferent attitudes towards the watershed programme.
5. The proper record was not maintained for watershed activities. The approach was to complete the targets and spend the amount on different activities as decided under the project. Thus, efforts made did not serve the purpose. It was simply a completion of project targets, whether it is needed or not and there was no attempt to learn and improve. The completion of targets also forced the field staff to sideline the guidelines.
6. There were man made as well as natural causes for making technologies inappropriate. The needs and aspirations of farmers were ignored and there was lack of integration among adopted technologies.
7. Managing the appropriate resources for technology adoption, technology demand of the society, unrealistic expectation of village people, lack of planning, untimely availability of required inputs for technology adoption, technological preference of local people, lack of identification of critical stages of work and training of labours were important technological concerns observed in adoption of technologies.
8. There should be appropriate flexibility in utilization of funds in guidelines. It was seen that due to rigidity in guidelines most of the money could not be utilized.

The results indicated that due to poor management and lack of supervision, appropriate technologies did not get through and as a result, farmers lost confidence in technologies and ultimately faith in programme. Tractors were used to carry out the work which was to be carried out through local labours. So the message of guidelines was modified to their own benefit and feasibility. There was no discussion on the utilization of technological inputs. It was decided and implemented by *mitra kisans* without consideration of farmers' suggestions and their cooperation. The farmers in general were found looking for the cash/kind benefit from the project. Further, the farmers were practicing several indigenous technologies which were not taken into account in the programme. The farmers' opinion about acceptance of technology was also found negative in few cases.

The study suggests that there were several man made and natural reasons for technological failure. There was no integration among adopted technologies. The views and opinions of farmers on the technological issues should be given due attention. This demands a bottom up planning approach, which was lacking in the project. This might be due to lack of experience in staff and non-consideration of location specific technological need.

(IV) Socio-economic Issues in Implementation

1. Selection of suitable persons for training was very important. It was found that personal contact, target fulfilment and other considerations were taken into account while selecting people for training. The trainees were selected on sympathetic ground to give honorarium. The practical utility had little concern in the selection of trainee. As a result, training imparted was unutilized. Lack of awareness in people about training programme was also there.

2. Corruption, vested interest of *mitra kisan mandal* (MKM), involvement of cash, dominance of influential people, lack of interaction among MKM members were other important issues observed in watershed project implementation.
3. Farmers had different perception of watershed project and as a result there was poor participation in the project. This perception needs to be changed by persuasion. "This is government programme" was common feeling, so village people destroyed some of work under project.
4. The project staff was not properly trained on participatory methodology. They should be adequately trained to resolve several issues through participatory action i.e. community sanction or fine.

After implementation of the project several conflicts emerges among people in project area but due to lack of conflict resolutions mechanism especially through meetings people had a wrong message of the programme. It shows that lack of interaction among society member, improper distribution of inputs, conflict among the farmers over sharing of common benefits, low status of women in society were the important issues needed to be resolved. Farmers thinking for development was individualistic and rarely follow group approach.

C. Perception of Project Personnel

1. The majority (67 %) of the project staff had graduate level education either in agriculture or agriculture engineering. Agriculture engineering graduates had technocratic mentality and was poor in group mobilization at field level as compared to agriculture background people. The personnel were categorized under work experience of 1 to 15 years. It was also

observed that project staff was not very much clear to express their actual length of service in watershed development. This was due to the doubt whether the experience of soil and water conservation and watershed development to be same or different.

2. More than 85 per cent of project staff had correct perception of objectives of watershed development project. They gave holistic meaning of watershed development. Only 15 per cent of them could not respond correctly and they had partial understanding of the watershed development. As a whole, the objectives of watershed project were perceived adequately by all.
3. As many as 66 per cent project personnel were not aware to any successful watershed project of the country.
4. In totality, project personnel had more importance to conservation and production components and less to socio-economic and management components. They had varied perception on socio-economic and management aspects but had high value towards integrated and holistic development of project.
5. The project staff involved was not clear about their nature of job they were to perform. The project personnel had little involvement in important activities of project. The personnel were found to be engaged in mobilizing farmers, training and coordination and in resource conservation and production measures.
6. The training imparted to project personnel had no practical utility. It was theoretical but to be actual field oriented. Therefore, it did not help in effective management of different activities of watershed projects. About 63 per cent project personnel were trained either from agriculture university or in workshop organized by the State department. They

perceived that the training for the project personnel should be organized at village level (55.71%), watershed level (31.42%) and district level (21.42%). The majority (77.14%) perceived that maximum emphasis in training should be on behavioural aspect and problem solving.

7. Organizational factors such as lack of proper training of grassroot workers, non-consideration of farmers needs, knowledge and suggestions, poor coordination among line departments, professional ego and commitment as reported by 35.71, 21.42, 18.57 and 18.57 per cent of project personnel respectively were considered as important factors responsible for people's participation.
8. Programme related factors, as project staff perceived in people's participation were watershed as a new project with unique objectives and approach (22.85%). They were not used to such work. About 20 per cent of them perceived that programmes would not provide immediate and direct benefits. They also perceived that programme could not be implemented without the help of contractors.
9. Socio-economic factors such as illiteracy and poverty in the society negatively affected the psychology of village people and their participation. The awareness about objective and benefit of the watershed programme was lacking as reported by 47.14 per cent. About 28.57 per cent reported that the village people had lost their faith in government system due to their past experiences and they were demotivated, prejudiced and suppressed as reported by 17.14 per cent. To improve the situation, project personnel suggested education about programme (38.57%) and use of participatory rural appraisal (PRA) techniques (10%) is essential.

D. Issues from Scientists

Scientists were not directly involved in programme implementation. Majority of scientists showed their concern on wrong execution of project without associating people in planning and development process. Most of them observed lack of co-ordination amongst multi-sectional departments for watershed project due to policy, professionalism and ego problem of the staff, and scientists perceived that there was lack of trained, motivated and good staff for watershed development programme. The same old staff of soil and water conservation was directed to carry out this work and hence, the programme could not yield.

Scientists felt that the watershed programme was target oriented and its contents were often guided from the top. They realized that the programme required a need based village level people's approach. This would ensure people's involvement in implementation process. They suggested that there should not be sectorial funding for achieving physical targets. They found that in the programme, the people's participation had no priority, which was the basic requirement of watershed development.

It was apparent from socio-economic factors that "people were illiterate and need proper training " was the major issue as perceived by the scientists. The other important issues were related to resource poor condition and want of immediate economic benefits, proper efforts and time in persuading farmers and urban effect in rural areas.

E. Performance of Non Government Organisation

The reasons for success of a Non Government Organization (NGO) in watershed were many. The important reasons were small organizational structure, strict supervision, good facilities for staff especially to visit the farmers but less salary, division of labour, better coordination in team, flexibility in policy and linkage with development department, incentives to good worker, and frequent evaluation.

Technologically, NGO was not sound but had better approach for technology dissemination. At village level informal groups and regular night meetings of farmers' with music, good training facilities with better use of audio-visual aids, convincing the farmers through role playing were the specific reasons to recognize with.

Conclusions

1. The analysis revealed that contractors were selected as *mitra kisans* and they were the major source of awareness for the farmers. Mass media had poor role in awareness generation.
2. The overall awareness of programme was observed to be low, which means farmers were aware to few activities. The awareness among the farming community about the project was maximum for soil conservation followed by pasture development, crop production and animal husbandry component, respectively. Among soil conservation, bunding and vegetative measures were most aware activities. Tree plantation on pasture lands (70 %), distribution of high yielding variety (HYV) seeds (40%) and the cattle fair (53%) were other activities of awareness to people.
3. The organizational issues in project implementation observed at field level were that the people working as contractors were also acted as *mitra kisans*. The next issue was about the expectations created in the beginning at farmers meetings, which gave rise to wrong message about the programme in the society. Conflicts between *mitra kisans* and project staff especially on payment observed as third major issues as reported by 47 per cent of respondents. At the time

of selection of *mitra kisans*, democratic process was ignored and personal relations dominated.

4. The organizational issues in project implementation observed at agency level were delay in payment due to complex procedure and policy of wrong mechanism of fund flow system (73.33 %). There were few good workers in the staff but due to frequent transfer (60.00%) the programme had to suffer, especially the faith of farmer in the project was lost. The organizational values were deteriorating fast. Poor coordination in multi-disciplinary team and unavailability of transport was also observed. The planning was not according to farmer's need and it depended on availability of funds in programme.
5. The appropriate technologies in absence of proper management was proved ineffective and, thereby, created poor impression among the farmers. Invariably, the farmer's suggestions and indigenous knowledge were found to be ignored by *mitra kisans* caused lack of interest of farmers in project implementation.
6. In society the conflict over sharing common benefits, selection of beneficiaries, problem in convincing the people, negative attitude towards government works were also the important issues which affected implementation of project.
7. The study revealed that majority (67%) of project personnel were graduate with 1-15 years of experiences in soil and water conservation, but most of them were not aware to any successful model watershed project. However, in general majority (85%) were aware of the watershed project objectives. The agriculture graduate had better approach for group mobilization whereas agriculture engineering graduate had technocratic attitude.
8. The project staff involved was not clear about their

nature of job they were to perform. The personnel was found to be engaged in mobilizing farmers, training and coordination and resource conservation and production measures.

9. About 63 per cent project personnel were trained for watershed development either from agriculture university or in workshops organized by the States department. However they perceived that the training for the project personnel should be organized at village level (55.71%), watershed level (31.42%) and district level (21.42%). The majority (77.14%) perceived that the maximum emphasis in training should be on behavioural aspect and at problem solving.
10. The reasons for lack of people's participation in watershed management programme was primarily due to the fact that there was no training of grass-root workers (staff members and *mitra kisan*) as reported by 35.71 per cent. The needs, knowledge and suggestions (21.42%) of farmers were not considered and incorporated in the programme was another factor in people's participation.
11. The programme is different from previous schemes (22.85%) and about 20 per cent of them perceived that this programme would not provide immediate and direct benefits. Further, the organizational structure of project itself invites the involvement of contractors (17.14%) and this was observed the major cause of concern lacking to people's participation in programme.
12. The farmers had no knowledge of benefits of the programme reported by (47.14%) and they also lost their faith (28.57%) in government system due to its previous functioning (28.57%) were other factors in participation. The general prevailing illiteracy (60%) and poverty (45.71%) prevented people for

interaction in meetings. To improve the situation, education about programme (38.57%) and use of participatory rural appraisal (PRA) techniques (10%) were suggested by project personnel.

13. Scientists were not directly involved in programme implementation, had perceived that the important cause for poor performance in watershed programme as improper execution (46.66%) and lack of coordination (31.11%) in departments due to professionalism and ego problem were the other reasons. Sometimes lack of trained, motivated and suitable staff was another major issue. They also expressed their views that programme was target oriented and content guided from top (20%) had no relevance to field situations. They realized that the programme required a need based village level people's approach. This would ensure people's involvement in implementation process. It was apparent from socio-economic factors that people were illiterate and they need proper training, poor resources and want of immediate economic benefits.
14. The reasons for success of a Non Government Organization (NGO) in watershed were its small organizational structure, strict supervision, good facilities for staff especially to visit the farmers, division of labour, better coordination in team, flexibility in policy and better linkages with development departments.
15. Technologically, the staff of NGO was not sound. They had poor knowledge of source of technology but had adopted better approach for technology dissemination. At village level, informal groups were developed and *choupal* of farmers with music were regularly organized. The organization had good training facilities with better use of audio visual aids. The trainers had the experience and capability to

convince the farmers through a number of cases resembling to rural scene.

Recommendations

1. Lack of awareness was the main cause for poor performance of watershed project. Therefore, maximum efforts are required to properly aware and educate the people about the project and its benefits and develop their leadership/institutions to take initiative in the project.
2. The activities of watershed programme and its benefits to rural people should be adequately made clear. For awareness generation NGOs methedology, use of audio-visual aids, regular farmer's meetings, use of local occasions and markets days for information dissemination, youths and adults involvement must be promoted.
3. The participatory planning and implementation of watershed project is the core point for the success. The project staff should be appropriately trained on the PRA techniques and its practical use. The starting point should be the rapport building followed by empowerment and mobilization to take initiate individually as well in groups. The PRA techniques must be conducted in advance and special budget provision in guidelines to be made as one component.
4. The training of grassroot level workers were essential. Training should be in participatory mode on continuous basis based on local needs and expectations. The location of training should be the village and watershed area.
5. The farmers in general were resource poor and illiterate in watershed areas. The watershed activities providing immediate benefits i.e., crop production, irrigation etc. should be given priority. This may help in confidence building and ensure people's

participation in the activities of the programme. All components should be adequately emphasized rather only soil and water conservation aspects.

6. The village panchayat should be taken into confidence by *Mitra Kisans Mandal* (MKM). The responsibility of planning and implementation of the project should be given to the village people through village panchayat. The social disputes, needs to be properly resolved by the active involvement of the people and imposing social code and conduct by the village panchayat. If required local constitution to be developed and followed strictly.
7. The implementing agency and staff should improve its credibility among farmers. To do so, the attitudes of staff towards farmers needs to be changed. The dedication to work and commitment to village people should be prerequisites for successful implementation of project.
8. The personal policies of staff i.e., transfer, promotion and salaries needs modifications. These items directly affect the motivation of staff on the job. The field level staff those initiated the programme should stay up to follow up of work. They should be supported by incentives, training and facilities of transport.
9. Organizing visits of farmers and project staff to model watershed project has great value in awareness generation and motivation about the project. Once or twice in a year, such visits will help to motivate and involve the people in the project.
10. Involvement of migrated city / town based people for their own village development should be encouraged through some mechanism. Their experiences should be taken in developing the programme.
11. Size of the watershed should be manageable with inclusion of few villages to develop as model project. Duration of project completion should not be

predetermined as these projects have their own gestation period to show the impact. However, participatory development approach may help to carry out and complete the targeted activities and it will be sustainable.

Future Course of Action

- Leadership dimension is important area for future research in watershed development project. How we should work and concentrate on development of human resource and social aspects in watershed area needs special attention for the success of the project.
- Special training methodology to educate the grass root level workers and village people for participatory resource conservation is to be evolved.
- The prescribed mechanism of *mitra kisan mandal* and local self-help groups is very vital in watershed development. How to check rural educated and uneducated youths from migrating towards cities and assign responsibilities of village development are very important. A thorough enquiry is required to understand their group dynamics for effective work at village level.
- Students of Ph.D need to be attached formally for their research project through inbuilt mechanism with national or State government agency. That would give practical benefit of work to both the organizations.

APPENDIX

Schedule for Data Collection

PART – I
Schedule for Farmers

Name .... *Age*............................ *Village*..................

1. Do you know about watershed scheme is being implemented in your area? Yes /No

2. What is that?

3. Name the activities of watershed project being implemented so far.
   1.
   2.

4. How do you come to know about the project? (*Mitra Kisan*, Project personnel, Panchayat members, Mass media, if others specify)

5. Do you have your land in watershed if yes, how many hectares

6. Do you heard about *Mitra Kisan*? If yes, what is their role in the project?

7. Have you attended any meeting of the programme? (If yes, where and what had been discussed?)

8. What problems have been observed in implementation of project?

9. Have you attended any training programme in the project, if yes; give the details :

   Place :
   Duration :
   Problem faced :
   Suggestions :

10. What are your problems of soil and water conservation?

11. How you benefited with programme?
    1.
    2.
12. What were your expectations from the watershed programme?

13. Name few indigenous practices being followed in agriculture.

PART – II
Schedule for Mitra Kisans

Name ....*Age*................ *Education*.............*Village*..........

1. How you have come to know about project and what were the points for discussion?

2. How and when you have been selected as *Mitra Kisan*?
   1.
   2.

3. People of the village are aware that you have been nominated as *Mitra Kisan*?

4. How you are educating/convincing the village people?
   1.
   2.
5. Farmers are cooperative to you, give your opinion?

6. Project personnel are cooperative to you, if not why?

7. What were the problems experienced in implementing the programme?

8. What have been your role in the project?
   1. 2.
   3. 4.

9. Have you received any training in project?

   Duration :
   Selection procedure :
   Problem faced :
   Suggestions :

PART – III
Schedule for Project Personnel

A. Schedule for Project Personnel

Name ....*Education*.........................*Institution*..................

1. What is your experience in watershed development project— Years

2. What is watershed development?

3. Why people's participation is poor in the programme?

   1. 2.

   3. 4.

4. How people's participation can be improved in programme?

5. How (activities) you are associated with watershed development?

6. Have you received any training under project, if yes?

   Where :
   Duration :
   Experience :

7. How training should be for this programme?

8. Any other suggestions for improvement in project?

B. Schedule for Project Personnel at Field Level

1. Explain the beginning of the watershed project?
   Selection of watershed project :
   Benchmark survey :

2. How you approach for people's participation for implementation of project?

3. How meetings conducted at village level with farmers and what was response of farmers during meetings?

4. What procedure followed in selection of *mitra kisans*?

5. What are your experiences in approaching people at field level?

6. Do you get farmers cooperation, if not why ?

7. What difficulties you had felt in implementation of project?

8. What you will say about multidisciplinary approach of work?

9. What are your experiences about project guidelines?

PART – IV
Schedule for Scientists/Experts involved in Watershed Development Research

Name ....*Designation*.......................*Institute*..................

1. Since how long you are working on watershed development. ....years

2. Are you aware about National Watershed Development Project for Rainfed Area (NWDPRA) . Yes/No

3. What type of approach being followed for watershed development? Sectorial/Holistic

4. What you will say about composition of the project?
   1.
   2.

5. It is said that project is not accepted by people, what are your comments?
   1.
   2.
6. What is your opinion about organisational procedure adopted for implementation of project?
   1.
   2.
7. What are your suggestions for success of the project?

PART – V
Schedule for NGO Personnel

Name ....*Age* ....*Education*.....................

1. Give the background of your organisation?
   Historical background :
   Aims and Objectives :
   Programme and Schemes :

2. How is infrastructures and other facilities of your organisation?

Staff	Transport
Training facilities	Laboratories
Accommodations facilities	Salaries of staff

3. What are the sources of funds for programmes?
4. Have you developed linkages with other organisations?

5. What problems are you facing in the organisation?

6. When you joined the organisation?

7. Is there any scheme on watershed development in your organisation? If yes give details.

   Activities :
   Organisational system :
   Multidisciplinary team position :

8. What problems you had faced in implementing the activities of watershed project?

9. How you are conducting training for farmers as well as for farm women?

10. What you will say about your job satisfaction?

11. Farmers were cooperative to you or not?

Bibliography

Anderson and Lorch (1994) : *Poverty; Agriculture Intensification and Environment*, B.P. Pal Memorial Lecture, IARI, New Delhi.

Akong, J. and O. Chitere (1991) : *Participatory Action Research in the Development Process working with Rural Communities : A Participatory Research Perspective* (ed.), pp. 57-66 in Kenya Nairobi Uni. Press.

Angeles Ms-de Los (1985) : Economic and social impact — analysis of an upland development projects in Nueva Ecija, Philippines, *Journal of Philippine Development* 12:2, pp. 324-394.

Anonymous (1991) : *A Collection of Proceedings of Seminar at WTC*, IARI, New Delhi.

Anonymous (1995) : During the discussion with technical staff of DPAP and DDP Programme at CGO Complex, New Delhi.

Bagchee, A. and S. Bagchee (1992) : Improving rainfed farming system through watershed development : A Case Study of Ralegaon Siddhi *J. of the Asian Farming System Association* 1:3, pp. 371-383.

Babu, R. and B.L. Dhyani (1994) : Socio economic aspect of watershed management programme in India, CSWCTRI Dehradun, *8th ISCO*, New Delhi.

Bali, J.S. (1987) : Agro industrial watershed for removal of poverty , *ISWC*, 31(2) : pp. 98-105.

Bhatta, B.D. (1982) : Implementing decentralization policies and programme : A Case Study on Rapti , IRDP. pp. 61, *BIDS Center for Eco. Dev. and Ad.*, Kathmandu , Nepal.

Bhusan, Brij (1994) Role of voluntary organizations in natural disaster reduction, *Swasth Hind*, Vol. 38th, No. 2 : 45.

Boyle, W.P. (1984) : *On the Analysis of Organisational Culture in Development Project Planning*. Working paper cooperative agreement on human settlements and natural resource systems analysis, Institute for Development Anthropology, USA.

Choudhery, Q. A. (1986) : Rural poor participation and small watershed projects in Bangladesh— A case study, *Journal of Local Governments*, 15 : 1, 139-153, BIDS.

Contrears, A. (1976) : Ref in Ronnide Camino Velozo (1987) Incentives for community development in conservation programme, FAO, *Conservation Guide*-12.

Deshpande, R.S. and Reddy V.R. (1991) : Differential impact of watershed based technology: some analytical issues. *Ind Jr. Agri Eco.*, 46 (3) pp. 261-269.

Dey, B.K. (1994) : Organizational mission: elusive concept and neglected practice, *Indian J. of Pub. Ad.*, Vol. XI : 15.

Draper, J.A., Nair M.D., Hain, Robert C. (Eds.) (1984) : *Voluntarism in Canadian Human Service, Issues in Canadian Human Services*, Toronto : Ontario Inst. for Studies in Education.

Gregerson, (1978) Ref in Ronnide Camino Velozo (1987) : Incentives for community development in conservation programme, FAO, *Conservation Guide*-12, pp. 43.

Grow, DD and Morss, ER (1988) : The notorious nine: critical problems in projects implementation, *World Development*, v., pp.16 :12,1399-1418; 62 ref., 3 tables.

Gupta, A. (1980) : *Proceedings of national seminar at soil and water conservation department*, Ministry of Agril., Govt. of India.

Hazare, Anna (1995) : *A report from a NGO of Ralegaon Siddhi village*, near Pune in Maharashtra, India.

Herbeniak and Willam (1984) : Strategy implementation Macmillan Pub Company division Macmillan, Inc.

Hoare, P.W.C. (1984) : Improving the effectiveness of agril development: a case study from North Thailand, *Manchester Papers Dev*, No 10, 13-43 33 ref OAE

Honadle, G. (1984) Planning and management of rural development projects, *Rural Development in Asia and the Pacific*, Vol. 1.

ICRISAT (1977) : *Annual Report Patancheru*, Hyderabad.

Jaiswal, N.K; A.P. Parandare and A.K. Jaiswal (1985) : People's participation in watershed management : A case study of DVC, *Journal of Rural Development*; 4 : pp. 409-465.

Jaiswal, N.K. and A.P. Punudare (*1982*). Planning and management of watershed, *Journal of Rural Development*, 1 (5), pp. 661-705.

Jasset, E. M. *et al.* (1990) : *Peoples Participation project in Rushinga Distt. Mashona Land Central : A mid term evaluation report*, Consultancy Report Services, Zimbabwe Inst. of Dev. Studies, No.17, pp. 35.

Jayaramalah, K.M. *et al.* (1991) : Extension strategies for minimising production risk in rainfed agriculture : Extension strategies for rainfed areas, *ISEE*, New Delhi.

Jayaraman, T. K. (1982) : Evaluation of implementation phase of rural development projects: a case study, *Argil. Administration*, 10 : 2, pp. 85 -100 Oae

Jha, S.K.; Baldeo Singh and R.P. Singh (1993) : *Utilisation of Indigenous Knowledge for Sustainable Mixed Farming*, Paper presented in "Congress on traditional science and technologies of India", IIT Bombay.

Joshi, A.L. (1994) : Peoples participation in soil conservation and watershed management in Nepal, Paper presented in *8th ISCO*, New Delhi.

Kanwar, J.S. (1991) : Indian agriculture at cross roads challenge and strategies. *XXII Lal Bahadur Shastri Memorial Lecture*, IARI, New Delhi.

Kerlinger, F.N. (1983) : *Foundation of Behaviour Research*. Surjeet Pub., Delhi, India.

Khosho, T. M. and K. G. Tejwani (1993) : Soil erosion and conservation in India, in *World Soil Erosion and Conservation*, edt. by David Pimental, Cambridge University Press, pp. 109-145.

Kohli, Uddesh (1979) : Implementation planning, *Yojana* , 16 June, pp. 13-17.

Koons, A. S. (1988) : Communication in the agriculture developments : A Cameroonian example: *Dissertation Abs. International, A humanities and social sciences 1988*, 49, 2, pp. 286, Diss. The American University from Microfilms Centers.

Krishnamachari, V.T. (1961) : The responsibilities of Panchayati Raj, Oct Symposiam, *Kurukshetra.*

Krishna, A. and Hedge (1994) : Integrated watershed development, a holistic approach to resource conservation : *Indian Farming;* Dec. pp. 25-30.

Lawrence, G. Herberniak and William F. Joyce (1984) : *Implementing Strategy*, Macmillan Pub Company.

Livingstone (1979) : Quoted in George N.D. rural development planning sectorial coordination *Vs* integration, *Yojna*, Oct. 5 , 1994, pp.15.

Mae Neil, T. (1980) : Adult education and voluntary organization, *Learning*, Vol. 3, No. 2, Fall.

Manage (1994) : MANAGE, *Extension Digest*, 2 (4): pp.1-18.

MANAGE Scientist (1994) : Watershed management, *Extension Digest*, MANAGE, Hyderabad.

Morris and Hough (1987) : The anatomy of major projects, *Johan and Sons;* Singapore.

Morris, Debbie (1996) : Using competency development tools as a strategy for change in the human resource function— A case study, *HRM* , Spring ,Vol. 35, No 1, pp. 35 -51

Mukhopadhayay, A. K. (1979) : Some reflection's on the role of Panchyatraj bodies in rural development in a block of A. P., *Economic Affairs* 24 : 5/7, pp. 119-183.

Muthaya, B.C. and S.V. Rangacharyulu (1980) : Relationship between faith in people and opinion on democracy, *Behavioural Sciences and Rural Development* 3 (2), pp. 140-44.

Narshimham, B. (1994) : Realising appropriate land use: *Indian Farming*, Dec., pp. 57-64.

Naidu, V.J. (1992) : Ref. in planning and peoples participation India, *Monthly Commentary* ,Jan., pp. 22-23

Narayan and Prasad (1989) : Soil and water conservation for better land water management, *Indian Farming,* Oct. pp.18.

Oermann, C. (1994) : How can planning by objectives be married to *Action Research,* Better News, No-1, pp. 8-13

Osterman, D. *et al.* (1989) : Coordinated resource management and planning : the case of the Mission flat Creek watershed, USA, *J. of Soil and Water Conservation* 44:5, pp. 403-406.

Purohit, S.D. (1994) : *Evaluation of NWDPRA : A Study of Two districts in Rajasthan,* Agro-Economics-Research Centre, Sardar Patel University, No. 90, pp.104.

Ramreddy, G. and Hargopal G. (1985) : *Public Policy and the Rural Poor in India: A Study of SFDA in A.P. Cess—* Research Studies Center for Eco and Social Studies Hyderabad, No. 1, pp. 319, BIDS.

Rao, Sunder (1988) : Impacts of dryland agriculture technology in Chevella and Pothulaguda model watershed development project in Medak dt, A.P. *M.Sc. Thesis,* A.P.A.U, Hyderabad.

Reddy, Y.U.R and T.S Walkar (1987) : Impact of watershed programme on the economic conditions of rural people, *Annual Report;* CRIDA, Hyderabad.

Raij (1987) : Soil water conservation in Sub-Saharan Africa : the need for a bottom up approach, *ODI,* Landon.

Richter, L. (1985) : Integrated rural developments—an overview of ILO experiences, No. 14, 311-328, *OAE* Hemberg German Federal Republican Vertigo Weltarchi, GmbH.

Sanders, D.M. (1985): Quoted in research on farmers motivation is key to future : An FAO view world association of soil and water conservation, *News Letter,* Vol. 2.

Sanghi, N.K.; Kerr and Sharma (1994) : Soil and water

conservation work with and learning from farmers in A.P., *Indian Farming*, Dec., pp. 57-64

Santhanam, M.L.; C.Y. Sastry and S. Vijay Kumar (1982) : Human and social factors in people's participation, *Journal of Rural Development*, 1(5) pp. 770-831.

Schneider and Snyder (1994) : Some relationship between job satisfaction and organizational climate quoted in *IJPA*, Vol. XL : pp. 29.

Schumacher, E.F. (1973) : *Small is beautiful: A Study of Economics as if people Mattered.* Blond and Briggs Ltd. London, p. 62

Sharma, S.C. and R. Hooja (1981) : Watershed management and peoples participation. *Kurukshetra*, 29: pp. 7-10.

Siddarmaish, B.S. (1991) : Attitude and adoption behaviour of farmers towards watershed mangement ; Extension strategies for rainfed areas, *ISSE*, New Delhi.

———, (1984) Peoples participation, Some psychological dimensions, *Journal of Rural Development*, 3 (4), pp. 249-329.

Singh, A. (1991) : Watershed as a means for land and watershed management—some experiences, WTC, IARI, New Delhi.

Singh, D.V. and R. L. Verma (1995) : Integrated watershed development project (Hills) H.P: An appraisal *Kurukshetra* , March issue.

Singh, Katar (1986) : *Rural Development Principal, Policies & Management*, Sage Pub., New Delhi.

———, (1988) Managing dryland watershed development programme lesson of Karnataka experiences, Research paper, Institute of Rural Management India, No. 1, pp. 35.

Singh, R. (1994) : *Impact of NWDPRA in U.P.*, mimeo, p. 130, ISAE, agro-economic centre, Allahabad University.

Singh, R.P. (1991) : Reporter's report on watershed development in 51st Annual Conference of the Ind. Soc. of Agri. Eco, *Ind . Jr. Agril. Econ*, 46 (3): pp. 482-491.

Singh, Y. P. (1995) Informal discussion at IARI, New Delhi.

Sombatpaint, S. *et al.* (1993) Soil conservation and farmers acceptance in Thailand (edited), *Topics in Applied Resource Management in the Tropics,* Witzanhausen, Germany.

Speidel (1971) : Ref. in Ronnide Camino Velozo (1987), Incentives for community development in conservation programme, FAO, *Conservation Guide-12.*

Srinivasaramanujan, T.C.A. (1994) : The current rural development model — an assessment, *Kurukshetra;* Oct. pp. 37-40.

Suelzer, R. and Sharma K. (1987) : Working with people ; some experiences with the people centred approach in the Tinau watershed Nepal, SWISS association for Tech Assistance, pp. 121, Kathmandu, Nepal.

Swaminathan, M.S. (1998) : *Agriculture Today,* July-August pp. 4-7.

Swanson, E.W. (1988) : Information system implementation: bridging the gap between design and utilization (R.W. Irwin, Home Wood I.L. 1988) *Research Policy,* 17 (2).

Tejwani, K. G. (1992 a) : Training for soil water conservation (a neglected activity) paper presented in *8th ISCO,* New Delhi.

Times of India (1996) : Vanishing Water, April 1, pp. 10.

Tolley, G.S. and Riggs F.T. (Eds) (1967) : *Economics of Watershed Planning,* Iowa State Univ. Press.

Upadhaya, A .P. and S.L. Intodia (1995) : A study on integrated watershed programme in Tribal Area of Rajasthan for change crop production, *Krishi Samikcha,* Feb., pp. 432-36.

Vaidyanathan, A. (1991) : Integrated watershed development: some major issues. foundation day lecture, *SPWD,* New Delhi 6 (4): pp. 1-9.

Van den ban A. W. and H.W. Hawkins (1988) : Management of Ext Organisation, *Agriculture Extension,* Pub: Longman Scientific & Tech. New York, pp. 262.

Verma, C.V.J. (1980) : Preface . In seminar on strategy for MM & PP in implement of WMP, *CBI & P,* New Delhi.

Vohra, B.B. (1995) : Water Conservation-Value of local efforts *Indian Express*, July 3, pp. 8.

Wandersman, Abraham (1981) : A framework of participation in community organisation, *Journal of Applied Behavioural Science*, 17 (1), pp. 27-58.

Waterman Hrobert *et al.* (1980) : Structure is not organisation, *Business Horizons* Pub., London (Ref. in *Management* by Stoner).

Wetzel., J.H. (1957) : How a watershed works: Challenges of our watershed, *SCSI*, DVC, Hazaribagh, Bihar.

White, T.A. and Quim R.M. (1992) : An economic analysis of the Maissode, Haiti, integrated watershed management Project (IWMP).

Wyckoff, J.W. (1985) : Planning and Lands Development Projects, *Nomadic Peoples*, No. 19, pp. 59-70, 29 ref OAE.

Yin C. (1984) : *Statistical Methods in Research*. McGraw Hill, pp. 42-47.

Zoghy, S. EL *et al.* (1987) : Variables affecting popular participation in organisation and community development activities in the new desert communities in south Taharir, Ezypt, Desert Development Centre, *The American University* in Cairo.

Index